P9-DNA-036

THE
CHOCOLATE
CONNOISSEUR

FOR EVERYONE WITH A PASSION
FOR CHOCOLATE

Chloé Doutre-Roussel

JEREMY P. TARCHER/PENGUIN
a member of Penguin Group (USA) Inc.
New York

JEREMY P. TARCHER/PENGUIN
Published by the Penguin Group
Penguin Group (USA) Inc., 375 Hudson Street, New York, New York 10014,
USA · Penguin Group (Canada), 90 Eglinton Avenue East, Suite 700, Toronto, Ontario
M4P 2Y3, Canada (a division of Pearson Penguin Canada Inc.) · Penguin Books Ltd,
80 Strand, London WC2R 0RL, England · Penguin Ireland, 25 St Stephen's Green, Dublin
2, Ireland (a division of Penguin Books Ltd) · Penguin Group (Australia), 250 Camber-
well Road, Camberwell, Victoria 3124, Australia (a division of Pearson Australia Group
Pty Ltd) · Penguin Books India Pvt Ltd, 11 Community Centre, Panchsheel Park, New
Delhi—110 017, India · Penguin Group (NZ), Cnr Airborne and Rosedale Roads, Albany,
Auckland 1310, New Zealand (a division of Pearson New Zealand Ltd) · Penguin Books
(South Africa) (Pty) Ltd, 24 Sturdee Avenue, Rosebank, Johannesburg 2196,
South Africa

Penguin Books Ltd, Registered Offices:
80 Strand, London WC2R 0RL, England

Previously published in Great Britain in 2005 by Piatkus Books Ltd

Most Tarcher/Penguin books are available at special quantity discounts for bulk purchase
for sales promotions, premiums, fund-raising, and educational needs. Special books or
book excerpts also can be created to fit specific needs. For details, write Penguin Group
(USA) Inc. Special Markets, 375 Hudson Street, New York, NY 10014.

Library of Congress Cataloging-in-Publication Data

Doutre-Roussel, Chloé.
    The chocolate connoisseur : for everyone with a passion for chocolate / Chloé Doutre-
Roussel.
        p.   cm.
    Includes bibliographical references and index.
    ISBN 1-58542-488-9
    1. Chocolate.   2. Chocolate candy.   I. Title.
    TX767.C5D68   2006   2005055980
    641.3'374—dc22

Printed in the United States of America
10 9 8 7 6 5 4 3 2 1

Book design by Paul Saunders

For Marlies and Roger

Contents

Images and illustrations

Line drawings of chocolate bonbons, cocoa pods, chocolate bar, ballotin of chocolates and chocolatière scattered throughout © Amanda Loverseed.

Illustrations on pp: 23, 53, 55, 58, 85, 86, 87, 116, 192 by Rodney Paull.

Images on pp: 11, 57 © The Bridgeman Art Library.

Images on pp: 15, 59, 120, 140 © Mary Evans Picture Library.

Images on pp: 18, 114 © Corbis.

Acknowledgements

I WANT TO THANK MY dear friend chocolate, who has been my best friend (sometimes a she, sometimes a he), my companion for more than 25 years, and the source of much of my joy. As with people there are the good and the bad chocolates, the elegant and the vulgar, the honest and the cheats, and the jewels you keep as close to you as possible for the rest of your life. My best friend chocolate is always there for me, supporting me even when things go wrong.

Chocolate has shown me a path in life, a philosophy for living. Discovering the world of chocolate has given me the opportunity to learn about myself: what inspires me, what hurts and delights and surprises me. I am driven by an inner fire of curiosity and chocolate has helped me to know who I am and what I want my life to be.

Chocolate has enabled me to meet my best friends, the people who crossed my path thanks to chocolate. Even those who crossed my path and left remain with me, among my greatest treasures.

Chocolate is a magic wand for me, often a more powerful means of communication than words, because people drop their defences before chocolate and become like children again, vulnerable, open, and receptive.

· ACKNOWLEDGEMENTS ·

In thanking chocolate I am also thanking all the people who helped me to discover this brown gold – my mother for putting melted chocolate on my lips when I was a few weeks old, my friends who accepted my obsession and didn't try to limit my passion (and refrained from stealing my chocolates!).

Thank you to all the professionals who, over the past ten years, looked beyond this obsessive girl and saw my passion, commitment and curiosity. Thanks to Karen Evennett for her help with writing the book and Anna Crago for her impressive work and perspicacity. Deepest thanks to Steve de Vries, the most humble, generous bright chocolate connoisseur I have ever met. And thank you to my choco dream team, Jack and Hilary, for their constant cocoa-obsessive enthusiasm and support.

Introduction:
A passion for chocolate

*W*HENEVER I ASK someone about their favourite chocolate, I see their face light up and their eyes start to sparkle. I know then that my simple question has transported them to happy times, and happy chocolate memories. I know, from the look on their face, that they love chocolate.

This is hardly surprising – most people love chocolate (certainly few people hate it!). But to my mind, chocolate lovers fall into two categories:

- Those who are so wedded to their current favourites that nothing anybody says to the contrary will change their mind. They know what they like!

- Those who want to learn more. They either thank me for introducing them to a new friend, or decide they hate what I have given them – but set themselves the challenge of discovering why it is deemed so 'special'.

This book is for all chocolate lovers, but perhaps particularly for those in the second category – innate connoisseurs who are always on the lookout for the best.

I believe chocolate has reached a turning point in its history. All over the world, we are seeing the rise of chocolatiers (chocolate makers, melters and sellers) who are truly passionate about chocolate, and perfectionist about their work. These people are quietly revolutionising methods of producing chocolate, seeking out the best-quality cocoa beans, and making chocolate that may well taste *entirely* different to the chocolate that you currently know and love.

What I want to do is guide you through this chocolate revolution. You'll learn how chocolate is becoming a gourmet foodstuff, ranking alongside the finest wines, coffees, teas, cheeses and olive oils. You'll see how chocolate tasting is becoming as advanced an art as wine tasting, with connoisseurs discerning flavours such as 'mushroom', 'berry' and 'floral' in chocolate, and using wine terminology like 'cru', 'vintage' and 'terroir'. And you'll discover that as fine chocolate is taken more and more seriously, the market for it grows exponentially.

In my job – as chocolate buyer at Fortnum & Mason, London's famous department store – I increasingly see people coming in and asking for chocolate from specific plantations or made with a unique and sought-after variety of cocoa bean. This would have been unheard of in 2002 (though the revolution was already well under way in France). But now, even supermarket brands of chocolate are changing the way they package their product, so word is spreading fast.

I love the fact that chocolate is such an important part of so many lives, because this is fuelling the chocolate revolution. When someone tells me they 'love all chocolate', my heart begins to dance because I know that, as a chocolate lover, this person will be willing to give all chocolate a chance – and discover what the very finest chocolate has to offer.

In this book, I will explain how chocolate is made, tell you about good chocolate and bad, and most importantly, teach you how to taste chocolate, so you can begin to decide for yourself what the best chocolates are and which ones suit you best. True connoisseurs prefer bars or blocks of plain chocolate to filled chocolates, and I'll tell you why. Along the way I hope not only to introduce you to a few new favourites, but to open your eyes to a whole new way of seeing chocolate.

In my case, I 'saw the light' at a very early age. I was a fussy eater, growing up in Mexico with nothing but Nutella and dark chocolate thins to tickle my taste buds. While you learned it at school, I learned it the hard way: the poor countries that grow many of our most basic crops – rice, tea, coffee, tobacco, and cocoa – do not process them. And although Mexico is a cocoa-producing country (not to mention the birthplace of cocoa cultivation!), the only chocolate we could find was the over-processed, sugary type produced by multinational companies.

Even our Nutella and chocolate thins were imported treats that we either squeezed into our suitcases on our return from our annual trip to France, ordered from a European mail order catalogue, or implored overseas visitors to bring us. Chocolate was literally the 'sweetener' that made up for the fact that we children had to surrender our bedrooms to our overseas guests. As the whole family welcomed arriving visitors at the airport, we children would wait anxiously, our hearts racing, eager to see how much precious chocolate they had brought with them.

On one occasion I remember waiting for my mother in the arrivals hall at Mexico's international airport as she returned from a trip to Europe, her suitcase laden with precious Nutella. We watched as a customs officer interrogated her – and became gradually more horrified as we saw my mother spread Nutella over her face. When she reached us, we greeted her with admonishments for wasting precious milligrams of our favourite food. 'But it was the only way I could get it through customs,' she explained. 'The officer said I couldn't bring a food product into the country. I had to pretend it was a beauty mask for my face!'

At the age of 14, I moved to Paris and was suddenly exposed to a much wider range of chocolate. As far as my pocket money would allow me, I bought every new bar I came across, saving the wrappings, and comparing each new taste with those I already knew. From this early age I began writing my comments and primitive tasting notes about each different bar. At the start these were very simple. For instance, I might describe a bar as 'too sweet, light brown, strong artificial vanilla flavour, grainy'. But my notebook gradually filled up, and eventually I had the beginnings of a database that I added to daily, tasting and comparing chocolate each day before breakfast when, in my opinion, the palate is at its most fresh – a ritual I still practise today.

I bought up to 20 bars a week, and gained notoriety among my friends for my obsession. For my 20th birthday, my friends arranged a surprise party. At one point they blindfolded me and formed a circle around me. A voice instructed me to open my mouth, but before I did so my nose had already sensed the beloved smell of chocolate. So I opened wide and, one by one, 25 tiny pieces of chocolate were popped into my mouth with a request for me to identify the percentage of cocoa (the total percentage of cocoa butter *and* beans in a bar). I not only gave the percentage but also the name of the chocolate, its brand, and my opinion of it!

You may never have thought of chocolate in this way before. I hope that in this book I'll be able to share my passion for chocolate with you – and expand your chocolate horizons in the process.

THE PRICE OF PASSION

When I landed the job of chocolate buyer for Fortnum & Mason in 2003 I found myself catapulted into the media limelight as 'the girl with the best job in the world'. Every reporter who met me started their interview with the same words: 'You're so lucky!'

I can see why people think that... After all, I eat all the chocolate I like, and I am paid to travel around the world looking for the very best chocolate available. To anyone who loves chocolate, it must look as if I'm permanently lodged on a chocolate-mousse cloud nine!

However, I firmly believe that luck has nothing to do with it. It wasn't pure chance that put me in this position. I have had a true passion (or some might say obsession) for chocolate from childhood, and over time this kind of passion becomes the air you breathe, the energy that motivates you, an everyday quest.

It's comparable to a passion for music or literature. Just like connoisseurs of either art, I cannot stop fighting to learn even more. I want to know about every new development about chocolate as it happens. I do not wait for the press to publish the conclusions of a symposium. I try to attend the symposium myself, or find a close friend who shares my chocolate passion to do so. I do not wait for a company to ask me to visit a plantation, all expenses paid. I use my holiday quota, pay for my own ticket, and find my way to the cocoa plantations to see, ask and learn.

It's a lot of work, but it is endlessly fascinating. To me, this is what passion is all about.

In this book I'll take you through a brief potted history of chocolate, from its beginnings as currency to present-day trends. I'll dispel a few popular myths and give you my vision of the future of chocolate. In between, there are lots of exercises, games and questions aimed at helping you to build up your own chocolate likes and dislikes. Ultimately, you'll be able to pick the chocolate you feel like according to your mood, or the time of day, or whether you feel like milk or dark, a bar or a filled chocolate, something flavoured or plain, sweet or savoury.

So tuck in, and enjoy!

A BRIEF HISTORY OF CHOCOLATE

1000 BC Cocoa trees are growing wild in the Amazon and appear in etchings on Classic Mayan pottery.

600–1500 AD: The Mayas and Aztecs use cocoa beans as currency, and the rich make an exotic drink from them.

1517: The Aztec Emperor Moctezuma introduces Spanish explorer Hernán Cortés to his favourite drink, *chocolatl*.

1528: Cortés returns to Spain with cocoa beans and the equipment needed to make the chocolate drink.

1620–1650: The Spanish slowly introduce their secret ingredient to the rest of Europe – where it continues to be consumed as an expensive and mostly 'medicinal' drink, and a treat for the elite.

1650: The chocolate drink reaches England.

1652: London's first coffee house opens. Here, people could drink coffee, tea… and chocolate. Coffee was by far the cheapest of the three, so chocolate remained a luxury for the rich.

1693: A form of solid chocolate is developed for making the drink at home – but it's nothing like the smooth chocolate we eat today.

1765: Chocolate arrives in the American colonies and the first chocolate factory opens in Dorchester, Massachusetts.

1815: It becomes possible to separate cocoa butter during the production process (and the by-product of this is cocoa powder!).

1831: John Cadbury begins manufacturing drinking chocolate and cocoa in the UK.

chart continues

1847: A new process makes it possible to manufacture an edible, solid form of chocolate – and the first chocolate bar is created.

1866: Chocolate is used in France for medicinal purposes.

1875: The world's first milk chocolate is created.

1879: Conching (see page 16) is invented – leading to much smoother, more aromatic chocolate.

1894: The American company Hershey makes the first mass-produced, affordable chocolate bar.

1913: The first filled chocolates appear.

1925: Cocoa beans are traded for the first time as a commodity at the World Trade Center.

1930s: Famous candy bars such as the Mars Bar and Kit Kat are invented.

1920s–1980s: Chocolate remains largely static and although the products do not change, marketing becomes increasingly important.

1985: Brands like Valrhona start to create chocolate made from selected high-quality beans and regions – the revolution is beginning.

1989: Lindt launches a 70% bar – the first supermarket brand to promote cocoa percentage.

2004: Chuao in Venezuela becomes the first cocoa-growing region to be legally protected as a producer of named-origin beans.

2004: About 600,000 cocoa beans are eaten in a year. Only *five per cent* are used in quality bars.

The shaded areas are periods of major change in the world of chocolate.

CHAPTER 1

Chocolate past and present

ONCE UPON A TIME in a faraway land, there was a magic bean that could transform the life of anyone who came into possession of it…

The poor used it as money to pay for food and cloth, while the rich made it into an exotic drink that boosted their energy and put a spring in their step. Then, one day, the precious bean was carried thousands of miles across the sea to Europe, where it remained an aristocratic drink for centuries before finally being turned into a chocolate bar.

Today's chocolate retains its fairytale aura. Yet it's also abundant – accessible magic, if you like.

It is also coming into its own as a gourmet food – and when future chocolate historians look back, the start of the twenty-first century will be known as the chocolate revolution, when the quality of chocolate started to matter more than the quantity.

Becoming part of this revolution – developing the connoisseur's nose that will help you sniff out quality chocolate – does demand a bit of work. But don't let that put you off.

A huge part of it is chocolate tasting, so it's hardly a tortuous business. Moreover, the knowledge and pleasure you'll gain really will make it all worthwhile!

Let's start by going back to basics, and looking at some ways in which the humble cocoa bean gained its rightful place in history.

Chocolate as a drink

For nearly all of its 3,000-year history, chocolate has been consumed as a costly drink or as a health food – a far cry from the bars and filled chocolates we associate the word 'chocolate' with today.

The Mayas and Aztecs both traded with cocoa beans – such was their value – and the rich, who could afford to literally drink their money, used the beans to make a form of hot chocolate flavoured with spices (vanilla and chili peppers were popular, but other spices were also used) and enjoyed for the sense of well-being and energy it gave. Hot chocolate was the champagne of society weddings, and the drink was prohibited to commoners.

As today, the drink was best served frothy and, to achieve this (for the froth was considered a sign of quality), it was poured back and forth between two jars.

A sixteenth-century Mayan image of hot chocolate being poured between jars

To both the Mayas and the Aztecs, hot chocolate was thought to work some kind of magic – and it was treated with the utmost respect.

The Mayas had a cocoa god, and the drink was used in many of their rituals. A bride and groom would exchange it in their marriage ceremony, and children were often 'baptised' with cacao water.

The Aztecs, who used to make an annual sacrifice of their most beautiful slave, would serve chocolate to the elected victim to temper his melancholy in the final week before his execution.

When the Spanish invaded the New World in the sixteenth century, they too got to sample the drink – but its bitterness was a shock to the Western palate (in his *History of the New World*, published in 1575, Giralomo Benzoni described it as 'a bitter drink for pigs'), and it became the fashion to sweeten it with honey. It was this version of the drink that became a particular hit with the upper classes.

The Dominican friar Thomas Gage (1600–1655) tells a story of ladies living in San Cristobal de las Casas, Mexico, who claimed they couldn't get through a high mass at the cathedral without a fortifying cup of hot chocolate (brought to them by their maids). The bishop, outraged by the tea party going on in the congregation, banned the drink from the house of God. The ladies left his church – and the bishop was later killed … by drinking chocolate laced with poison.

When chocolate reached Europe, it remained a drink for the elite as it had been in South America. In these upper echelons of society, however, it began to take on the kind of simple social associations we recognise today – friends chatting over a cup of chocolate. In France during the time of Louis XIV, for example, it was a great honour if you were invited to drink hot chocolate – usually at around 10 am, while your host remained in bed!

In Spain today you can still buy grainy, sugary drinking chocolate in blocks, probably relatively unchanged since 1600. The country has retained its chocolate-drinking tradition and it's common to find it served midmorning with churros, straight-shaped doughnuts coated with sugar.

MEXICAN STREET CHOCOLATE – A TASTE OF HISTORY

If you have the opportunity of travelling to Mexico, go to the colourful street markets. You will find Indian women selling fist-sized tablets made from cocoa beans which have been pan-roasted at home, peeled by hand, roughly ground on a *metate* (a slab of volcanic stone used for grinding foods) and flavoured with cinnamon and a lot of sugar.

It is a far cry from what developed countries call chocolate. It doesn't melt, it is grainy, and it crunches with sugar crystals. It is, not surprisingly, very sweet. But these tablets are intended to be grated and then dissolved in hot water or milk to make a drink that hasn't changed much from the old recipe used by the Spanish in the sixteenth and seventeenth centuries. I grew up in Mexico, and when I return to visit my family, I still seek out the women selling their chocolate tablets in the market. I buy them for the simple pleasure of steeping myself in another culture, even though the flavour, to me, in no way replicates chocolate.

Although I really concentrate on pure chocolate bars and suggest that, as a budding connoisseur, you do the same, hot chocolate is a wonderfully soothing, pleasurable drink, and I have often served it at themed chocolate evenings for my friends. For my favourite recipes, see Chapter 5.

Chocolate as medicine

The Aztecs had taught the Spanish colonials that chocolate was healthy, and the drink was esteemed as a medicinal remedy when it reached Europe. Philip II of Spain's personal physician, Francisco Hernandez, recommended chocolate to cure fevers, cool the body in hot weather, and relieve stomach pains. People started to use it to aid digestion and, in 1650, when the drink reached England, it was advertised as 'curing and preserving the body of many diseases'.

In 1866 chocolate entered the French pharmocopia and apothecaries developed chocolate lozenges which they sold for their mood-enhancing or digestive properties. These were available in two flavours: plain, or with ingredients such as vanilla, pepper and cloves (which had their own medicinal qualities).

Today, chocolate is being heavily promoted as a health food – for its antioxidants and brain stimulants. (More about that in Chapter 8.) In the future, I'd like to see chocolate – that is, *real*, good-quality, high cocoa-content chocolate – being recommended by doctors for its pleasurable, anti-depressant qualities, just as they might recommend a glass of red wine to fight heart disease. Why? Because when you're happy, you're stronger in the face of illness. And I really believe happiness and chocolate go hand in hand!

Chocolate as a food

Today we associate chocolate with bars and filled chocolates, but as you have seen, these products only emerged relatively recently. Chocolate was a drink for most of its history, and the first (gritty) bar wasn't made until 1847.

During the time of the Industrial Revolution, chocolate bars became the product we know and love today – cheap and accessible to the vast majority. The key events were these:

- In 1815 a Dutch chemist called Van Houten started looking for a way to remove much of the fatty cocoa butter from chocolate, and eventually reduced it to a 20 per cent fat 'cake' that could be pulverised into a fine powder – what we call 'cocoa'.

- With this breakthrough, in 1847, Fry's in the UK found a way to mix a blend of cocoa beans and sugar with melted cocoa butter (the by-product of the defatting process) to make a viscous paste that could be cast into a mould. Voilà – the world's first chocolate bars!

DID YOU KNOW?

The Fry, Cadbury and Rowntree families of British chocolate fame were all Quakers. Many Quakers set themselves up in business and manufacturing, and chocolate seemed a good option. At the time it was viewed as a healthy and revitalising drink, and the Quakers wanted to make it available to people as an alternative to the more morally dubious alcohol.

- In 1867 Henri Nestlé, a Swiss chemist, discovered a way of evaporating milk to make a powder. In 1875 Nestlé and chocolate-maker Daniel Peter added this milk powder to chocolate to make the world's first milk chocolate bar.

- In 1879 Rodolphe Lindt invented a machine for 'conching' (a process by which chocolate is mixed for up to three days at a minimum of 10°F and a maximum of 167°F), which vastly improved the quality of chocolate confectionery: it helps aromas develop, acids to evaporate and the texture to become finer and smoother.

- By the 1920s, much of the world's chocolate was being made from cheap, reliable, but not very tasty beans called Forastero – a fact noteworthy mainly because it contributed to lower production costs. To improve the flavour of the Forastero bean, ever-increasing amounts of sugar and vanilla flavouring were added to the mix. Most of the chocolate we know today is made from this combination of workhorse beans and overpowering flavourings.

All these technological advances and other changes meant chocolate could be cheaply mass produced. From being a drink for the elite, it was now a readily available and affordable sweet. In 1893, a Belgian labourer would have had to work for 24 hours straight to afford a 7 oz block of chocolate – but by 1913 the price had come down so much that he'd only have had to put in 24 *minutes*. And today's mass-produced chocolate is even cheaper.

STILL GOING STRONG...

Van Houten is still a famous name for hot chocolate powder.

- Fry's Chocolates – perhaps now most famous for Fry's Turkish Delight, invented in 1914 – still steams ahead today, albeit as a subsidiary of Cadbury.
- Nestlé is now to Switzerland what Coca-Cola is to the US: a symbol of the Swiss way of doing things.
- Lindt still exhibits an early conching machine in its Zurich headquarters, and now manufactures and sells chocolate in 39 countries. What a success story!

So, amazingly, many of the key players in the nineteenth-century revolution of chocolate are still around today – and are still some of the best-known supermarket brands.

All these companies have done a huge amount to promote chocolate – but their products, while enjoyed by billions, will never be in the top league that is of interest to the connoisseur. They tend to be what I call 'candy' (a term used by

A 1893 poster for Van Houten by Adolphe Leon Willette

prenez du Cacao
Van Houten

Americans for their 'chocolate', which contains very little cocoa), heavily flavoured with sugar and artificial vanilla ('vanillin'). Unfortunately, this is a taste the world has come to associate with chocolate, but you may start to reject it once you have discovered what I call *true chocolate*.

Chocolate as a commodity

When Christopher Columbus encountered the cocoa bean six centuries ago, it was being used as currency to pay for everything from household groceries to domestic slaves.

A BEAN'S WORTH

Chocolate historians are fond of regaling their readers with stories about what one could buy with cocoa beans. According to Hernando de Oviedo y Valdez, who went to America in 1513 as a member of Pedrarias Avila's expedition, ten cocoa beans could buy the services of a prostitute – or your own slave. Four beans would get you a rabbit for dinner.

Reports about exactly how much things cost differ, but Michael and Sophie Coe, whose book *The True History Of Chocolate* I recommend to anyone interested in the intricacies of cocoa's past, found the following in a list of commodity prices in Tlaxcala, Mexico, in a document dated to 1545:

A small rabbit = 30 beans
An avocado, newly picked = 3 beans; a fully ripe
    avocado = 1 bean
One large tomato = 1 bean
A fish wrapped in maize husks = 3 beans.

It wasn't only as ancient currency that cocoa had any worth. Once chocolate gained mass popularity during the Industrial Revolution, cocoa beans were again worth their weight in gold, metaphorically speaking, as manufacturers couldn't get enough of them. At this time, as we've seen, many of the big names we know today began to emerge, and chocolate began to become a highly marketable commodity.

Today we hold continental chocolate-makers in high esteem – but we've forgotten why. Several Swiss companies made important technological advances and were once at the forefront of the industry, but have made no great strides since their heyday in the nineteenth century. In fact, their efforts have mainly concentrated on streamlining processes, creating cheaper, poorer-quality chocolate. Furthermore, how often have you heard people say that Belgium has the best chocolates? In my opinion, the country has earned its reputation mainly through marketing breakthroughs.

A brief history of Belgian chocolate

- Neuhaus developed the first chocolates that could be filled with creams (the famous Belgian moulded chocolates) and his wife invented the gift box, or 'ballotin', to sell them in.

- Leonidas leapt in with a much cheaper version of boxed chocolates, causing the quality and price of all chocolates to drop as everyone tried to keep up with them.

- Godiva (which despite its swanky image has been owned by the American food giant, Campbell's Soup, since 1974), simply marketed itself as selling 'The best chocolates in the world!' – and the slogan was enough to convince the public, who flocked to buy their chocolates.

When I took up my job as chocolate buyer for Fortnum & Mason, I introduced myself to my new staff by holding a chocolate workshop. I always start these sessions by asking the people gathered to reveal their favourite chocolate. More than one person volunteered that they loved Godiva, 'because it's the best chocolate in the world!' Some even added, 'I've never tried it, but I know.' That's what I call effective marketing!

Godiva is now perceived as one of the leading luxury brands. But Godiva isn't the only company with an effective marketing plan. My favourite example of the power of marketing is the Cadbury Creme Egg, probably as close to chocolate as a chicken's egg as far as I'm concerned!

Cadbury's marketing genius goes back a long way. In 1868 they produced the first decorated chocolate box. The attractive branded boxes could be kept long after the chocolates, and became one of the first chocolate marketing campaigns. Cadbury is still one of the world's biggest producers of chocolate, and remains the most popular bar in most of the English-speaking world.

The message I'd like you to take away from this is: the bigger the company, the bigger the marketing budget. Think of the best, tastiest and priciest olive oils or cheeses and they tend to come from 'boutique' companies – small groves or dairies that concentrate on quality ingredients and production values. I believe the same goes for chocolate.

Chocolate today

The world now consumes 42.2 billion dollars' worth of chocolate products – but most of this is milk chocolate or candy, satisfying a sweet tooth rather than a gourmet one. And most is now from the less flavoursome, but more robust, Forastero trees.

Because they are such big business, cocoa beans are exchanged as a commodity on the stock market. They're bought many years in advance to safeguard against fluctuations in the market price, and to maintain the ability to meet demand whatever unpredictable event occurs – be it a war, an economic crash, a cyclone or a disease.

The figures opposite show how much chocolate we eat, per head, per year in different countries. These figures take into account all chocolate, good and bad (including candy bars and other chocolate confectionery) – but lower-quality beans account for the lion's share. Think about how much chocolate you've eaten…did you know it's possible you have never tasted the best varieties of beans?

When you consider that 85 per cent of all harvested cocoa beans are Forastero, and look at the world's top ten selling brands, it is no surprise that most people have not yet encountered fine chocolate. In fact, the top sellers don't include anything that's 'real' chocolate – the list below is mainly candy with a thin milk-chocolate coating, except for Cadbury Dairy Milk. In fact, even that only contains 20 per cent cocoa – which, according to the EU, is not enough to make it officially chocolate!

The world's top ten chocolates

1. Mars Bar
2. Twix Twin
3. Snickers
4. Maltesers
5. Kit Kat (four-finger)
6. Cadbury Dairy Milk
7. Kit Kat Crunchy
8. Crunchie
9. Bounty Milk
10. Twirl

Once you've checked out the list above, it's hardly surprising that when chocolate lovers come to my workshops and

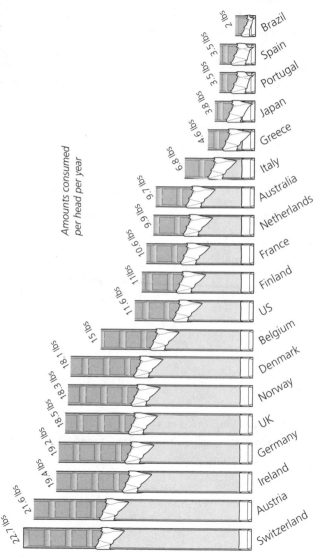

Amounts consumed per head per year

Who eats the most chocolate?

Brazil — 2 lbs
Spain — 3.5 lbs
Portugal — 3.5 lbs
Japan — 3.8 lbs
Greece — 4.6 lbs
Italy — 6.8 lbs
Australia — 9.7 lbs
Netherlands — 9.9 lbs
France — 10.6 lbs
Finland — 11 lbs
US — 11.6 lbs
Belgium — 15 lbs
Denmark — 18.1 lbs
Norway — 18.3 lbs
UK — 18.5 lbs
Germany — 19.2 lbs
Ireland — 19.4 lbs
Austria — 21.6 lbs
Switzerland — 22.7 lbs

explain what they like to eat and why they like to eat it, most are still into candy, rather than 'real' chocolate. They eat it because it makes them feel good, it cheers up a bad day, and it's a form of indulgence.

What we choose to eat is also often dictated by where we come from, as countries seem to have their own chocolate identities.

- *Belgium* is the country of big moulded chocolates, with creamy, soft fillings, and milk chocolate bars.

- *Austria and Germany* both favour chocolates filled with marzipan or hazelnut paste, and milk chocolate bars.

- *Scandinavians* are entrenched in their milk chocolate culture and also eat a lot of white chocolate.

- *France* is a mainly dark chocolate nation (in fact, dark chocolate is so popular in France that it's the only country in the world where Lindt's entire range of dark chocolate is sold!).

- *Spaniards*, true to their history, still prefer their chocolate in a mug.

- *Italians* love *gianduja*, a hazelnut and chocolate paste – Ferrero Rocher or Nutella are its most successful versions.

- *English-speaking countries* prefer above all milk chocolate (such is the legacy of Cadbury), white chocolate and big, round truffles.

- *The Japanese* also love milk and white exclusive chocolate, importing French chocolates in large quantities.

These tastes are dictated by tradition, and the taste of each culture runs the gamut of 'good' to 'bad'. What one generation enjoys is passed on to the next. It is a difficult cycle for those making 'real' chocolate to break. But it can be done. Anyone with a palate and the will to learn will find their way to appreciate fine chocolate.

Good chocolate in a nutshell

I've been talking rather a lot about 'real chocolate' – but what do I mean when I say this? You'll learn more in the next few chapters, but put very simply, there are a few basic criteria:

- High-quality beans and other ingredients, treated with care.

- Production methods aimed at extracting the most flavour from the bean.

- A reasonable level of cocoa content, so the cocoa is not drowned out by sugar or other flavourings.

'Real chocolate' is sold in two types of shops:

- In delicatessens, department stores, and some high-end supermarkets – bars and filled chocolates are mainly sold here.

- Own-name shops. Some of these have chains of shops (and their own factories). Others are less well known, have only one or a few shops, and have a lab out the back to create new products.

The difference is not so much about where the brands are sold, of course, but is more to do with their regard for quality. If you want to be ahead of the game, look out for small companies putting quality first and profits second. Their chocolates may be new to you now, but I promise that they will feel like old friends by the time you finish this book.

What makes these companies special? They care about the cocoa beans they use and where they are sourced and are prepared to pay more for good quality. Often, they use less high-volume machinery than the larger companies and spend longer extracting the aromas from the beans. And they are always on the look out for better raw ingredients and improved production methods.

All the fine brands mentioned below are distributed in specialist shops and department stores, and on the chocolate websites listed on pages 210–11.

- *Amedei* – an Italian chocolatier based in Pisa, Italy. In 1997, after visiting cocoa plantations in Venezuela, Amedei decided to produce chocolate only from beans personally selected at the plantations (rather than via bean-brokers). Their chocolate range has a wide choice of dark chocolate bars, and a few filled chocolates. They are the direct competitors of Valrhona (*see below*), but are a much smaller company. Amedei's Chuao and Porcelana bars are their jewels.

- *Bonnat* – a French company founded in 1884. Their first dark chocolate bars, made from beans from specific countries (Venezuela and Madagascar), were produced in 1902. They were the first to propose a range of bars at 75 per cent cocoa, each one made with beans from a different country. Their initiative has now been widely copied by other brands. In 1994, they were also the first to launch the concept of vintage in chocolate, with their Hacienda el Rosario bar, made from beans from a specific plantation. Their distribution is very limited thus the brand not very well known.

- *Chocovic* – an old company from Barcelona, which has been revived to follow the model of Valrhona, focusing on the world of professionals working with chocolate. Chocovic's cookery school has an international reputation. Their dark chocolate range Origen Unico is available in department stores and supermarkets.

- *Michel Cluizel* – a French brand from Normandy, which offers several different chocolate bars from specific cocoa plantations and a variety of boxes containing assortments of milk and plain chocolate, enabling you to discover the influence of bean origin or cocoa content on the taste of a chocolate. Their range competes directly with much older fine chocolate brands such as Valrhona. Try their Mangaro and Los Ancones bars.

- *Domori* – a young Italian company from Genoa. They co-own a big plantation in Venezuela. The founder is a passionate young agronomist who decided to revive the high-quality Criollo cocoa bean and since 1995 he has grafted various pure Criollo trees into different root stocks. Every year, they increase their range of top-quality bars. Their gems are the bars made with beans selected from specific areas of Venezuela, such as Esmeraldas, Porcelana and Carenero Superior.

- *El Rey* – were established in 1929 and in 1995 became the first modern chocolate plant in Latin America. Until

2004, El Rey chocolates were the only example of a relatively fine chocolate produced in the country of origin of its cocoa beans by a national company and distributed around the world. Colombia, with Chocolates Santander, has recently successfully reproduced the concept. The El Rey range is small, and all chocolates are made with a blend of beans from a region south of Caracas. The chocolate could be described as a cross between fine and mass-market chocolate.

- *Guittard* – a family-owned San Francisco chocolate manufacturer established in 1886. They mainly produce chocolate for professionals. In 2000 they launched a fine chocolate selection from small plantations around the world, which is distributed in speciality stores in the USA and overseas.

- *Marcolini* – a Belgian chocolatier famous for their range of fine filled chocolates. Since 2003 Marcolini have also been producing bars from cocoa beans from various plantations. Try their Ecuador and Java bars.

- *Michael Recchiuti* – a San Franciscan company melding American forward-thinking with European artisanal methods. Although he does not source his own cocoa beans, he uses only the finest raw materials. Try the 85%, the best high-cocoa percentage bar I have tasted so far.

- *Pralus* – a French company from Roanne, founded in 1948, which makes finest-quality chocolate using small batches of carefully selected cocoa beans. Pralus chocolates are the best way to discover that chocolate aromas can be as intense and complex as those in wine. With the

Java bar you will be surprised to encounter notes of wet wood, moss and wild mushrooms.

- *Scharffen Berger* – an American company that produces excellent cocoa powder and a wide range of chocolate bars; among the finest made in the USA. Try their limited edition Jamaica and Porcelana bars.

- *Valrhona* – a French company founded in 1924. They introduced the Gran Cru chocolate range, first in 1985 to the world of professional chocolatiers, then, in 1990, to all of us. This range of chocolate is made from the finest beans selected from geographic regions (for example, Caraïbe is made from beans from the Caribbean region; Manjari from Madagascar). Reliable, good-quality chocolate from a successful French company. Try their Manjari and Palmira bars.

Remember: small is beautiful! Don't be afraid to try an expensive new chocolate simply because you don't recognise the name on the bar – it may be made by a small manufacturer who cares deeply about his product, and has done his best to perfect it.

These quality brands are not easy to find – you may have to hunt hard or order from the internet (see Resources, pages 210–11). But I do urge you to seek them out. Only by doing so can you recognise and rule out any smartly labelled impostors – for the chocolate revolution will lead big manufacturers to try to cash in on chocolate's new gourmet status, with their own cheap versions. Novice connoisseur beware!

·

CHAPTER 2

Building your own chocolate profile

*Y*OU MAY LOVE chocolate…but how much do you *know* chocolate? To my mind, there is chocolate, and then there is *chocolate*. What you buy in the supermarket is a different proposition from the finest-quality bars you have to hunt for in department stores or delicatessens. Have you taken the time to sample good-quality chocolate yet?

To my mind, there are a few necessary ingredients that the budding connoisseur must possess. You need to be curious. And it's good to know what you like. This doesn't mean being closed off from trying new things – or stopping when you have found something you like. For me, being truly passionate about chocolate has been a lifelong quest. I like to explore new chocolate, give another chance to chocolate I have previously rejected as no good, compare different varieties, and question my own assumptions. I have a good idea of what I like, but I ensure that this doesn't close me off from trying anything new – although I do draw the line at boozy white chocolate truffles. Let's just politely say that these cause mutiny in my taste buds!

But what about you? If I were to offer you a new chocolate with the promise that it will taste unlike anything you have ever tasted before, would you be curious enough to try it?

If I were to tell you that there are chocolate bars that are as different from a standard bar as lemons are to mustard, or that some dark 75% chocolate bars are as smooth and mellow as milk chocolate, what would you think? Would you want to know more?

You may be about to encounter something wonderful that knocks spots off the chocolate you have loved for life. That can be daunting. This new chocolate may be more expensive or harder to find than you're used to. It may also cause you to reject a chocolate you've grown up with – a chocolate that holds all sorts of happy memories, and is your favourite comfort food… Nobody likes to say goodbye to an old friend, to explore alone an unknown path in life.

On the other hand, you may be about to discover that I am extolling the virtues of a chocolate you loathe. Will you wonder about the quality of your palate, or feel affronted that a so-called chocolate connoisseur chooses something you would not? Will you feel concerned at the new direction chocolate is taking?

I'd like to reassure you. Whatever kind of chocolate you're currently eating, and however you eat it – whether you snack on family-sized bars of milk chocolate, fantasise about Fererro Rochers, or selectively eat only 70% organic bars with your coffee – this book will help you to broaden your interest and expand your knowledge, and give you some tips on where to meet fellow choco-soulmates.

Knowledge, passion, curiosity, dedication – these are the steps along the way to becoming a chocolate connoisseur, even if you end up going back to your old favourite. You will at least know then why you stick to it and, having learnt to look at it in a new way, your pleasure in it will be much stronger. Your relationship with chocolate will have changed for the better!

Your next step is to start building your own chocolate profile. How far will you need to go in order to become a connoisseur? Are you halfway there already … or do you still have a lot to explore?

Your chocolate profile: step 1

The table opposite will help you to see at a glance what kind of chocolate you love most. What it also does, though, is to provide you with some ideas for what *else* you might like.

Look at the names of the bars, and circle those that you like or usually buy. Do they fall into any one category?

So what does it all mean? The distinction I've drawn here is a very simple one. Column 1 chocolates come from large companies and are available almost anywhere that chocolate is sold. The chocolates in column 2 are (yes, the bad news) more expensive, and are from my list of companies to watch out for – that is, typically, small ones who are doing amazing things with superb raw materials.

My ultimate aim is to show you that in time you can learn to love the very best milk or dark chocolate. You may have always eaten a bar available in any newsagents' shop – but now find yourself going for an artisanal variety in a big way. Or you may never have imagined yourself eating dark chocolate, until you encountered a truly ambrosial bar of it

	1	2
Milk		
	Cadbury Dairy Milk	Jivara (Valrhona)
	Galaxy	Milk (Amedei)
	Milka (Nestlé)	Lait Entier (Weiss)
	Milk (Lindt)	Latte Sal (Domori)
		Milk 41% (Scharffen Berger)
		Melissa (Pralus)
Dark		
	Lindt Excellence 70%	Manjari, Gran Couva
	Dark organic brands	(Valrhona)
	(70% or more)	Chuao, Porcelana (Amedei)
	Any dark bar from the	Java, Indonésie (Pralus)
	supermarket	Porcelana, Puertomar
	Bournville (Cadbury)	(Domori)
	Côte d'Or Noir	Chocolate and 'nibs' (Corallo)
	Duchy Originals	Bittersweet 85% chocolate
		(Michael Recchiuti)
		Mangaro (Michel Cluizel)

from column 2. See Chapter 4 for more recommendations for each type of chocolate lover.

You might notice that a few of your favourite things do not appear in the table above. Where are Mars Bars and white chocolate? Where are filled chocolates? Well, they're not there for a simple reason. When chocolate connoisseurs meet to taste and discuss *real* chocolate, they usually choose bars. It's the pure, unadulterated form of chocolate. White chocolate (which only uses the cocoa butter from the cocoa bean) doesn't count – and neither does the milk chocolate wrapped around candy bars. These products are more about the sugar and vanilla than the chocolate. A filled chocolate, packed with cream or alcohol, is nice – but put it in your mouth, and is it really the *chocolate* you're tasting, or the sugar and the flavourings? For a connoisseur, the bar's the thing ... just as a wine buff wouldn't spend too much time on a spritzer.

If your curiosity is piqued by all this, you'll find it leading you to seek out the best, and I suggest that you follow the recommendations given throughout this book at your own pace.

A CONSUMING PASSION

Compared with other gourmet pursuits – especially wine – chocolate is very affordable. This is a wonderful bonus, as I can think of nothing more frustrating than having a passion for something whose cost prohibits you from enjoying it to the full.

But this doesn't mean becoming a chocolate connoisseur is entirely without effort. You don't just waft into it: time, energy, imagination and a sense of adventure are all needed for this consuming passion.

Having a passion for *anything*, not just chocolate, is special. Many people feel that it has chosen them, rather than the other way round. It makes them feel alive: their passion is their oxygen.

Think of Ellen MacArthur, who at 28 broke the world record for sailing solo around the world. She began saving her lunch money to buy a boat when she was just eight years old. She was focused and dedicated, channelling all her spare time, energy and money into her passion. And it paid off.

My own passion led me to give up my well paid job as an agronomist and work unpaid for a chocolatier – but this was Paris's famous Pierre Hermé, the so-called 'Picasso of Pastry' (I didn't know this before I wrote to him, along with dozens of other chocolatiers). Working for Hermé at the renowned Parisian patisserie Ladurée, where he incorporated his wonderful chocolate into amazing cakes and pastries, was an honour, and the discoveries I made about chocolate were life-changing.

Through this job, I met people who shared my passion for the first time, much to my delight. M. Hermé introduced me to the finest chocolates, the raw materials used to make them, and the alchemy behind their combination. Not only did I learn a huge amount about what differentiates good chocolate from bad, I also found that the more I discovered, the more like minds I met, and the more my passion grew. There was, in short, no going back.

At this point in working out your chocolate profile, you might want to think about how big a part chocolate plays in your life.

Is it important, but a bit peripheral? No problem: even if you start by trying a new bar of chocolate once a week, or holding chocolate evenings with your friends every two months, your love for good chocolate will bring something special into your life.

If, on the other hand, you are like me, and chocolate is the main focus of your life, you may find you need to reassess your priorities to give it the space it needs.

But what if chocolate is definitely a passion – except it's got to be Galaxy, Mars Bars or Milk Tray? Don't worry. If you are keen to learn, you will. Remember, my own passion began with Nutella and Lindt chocolate thins all those years ago in Mexico. I loved them, and they became the springboard for my desire to explore every chocolate I could find.

Your chocolate profile: step 2

For fun, you could think back to your own chocolate history and palate development – and work out where you would like this book to take you. In my chocolate tasting courses, I always start with a round table, asking each person several questions to try and define their chocolate profile. How would you answer the following?

- What are your chocolate eating habits today? Do you eat filled bars, plain bars or filled chocolates?

- How do you eat chocolate – on its own, with coffee, after a meal?

- What brands of chocolate do you buy regularly?

- When do you eat chocolate? How often? Is chocolate a reward for you, a way to relax from stress, a way to fill boredom, or something else?

- Do you feel any guilt after you've eaten it, and if so, why?

- What kinds of chocolate do you like to get as a present (bars, or filled chocolates)?

- What chocolates did you have at home during your childhood? How have your chocolate choices changed since then?

- Can you eat a piece of chocolate without finishing the bar?

- What influences you when choosing chocolate?

- Do you make an effort to try new foods, or do you stick with what you know?

- Have you ever tried any of the brands on page 33? If so, what did you think?

I meet plenty of people through my workshops who have only ever eaten the 'column 1' chocolate from the chart on page 33. Usually, they'll stick to just a few brands. Yet these very people are often the ones who are most thankful for their discovery of real chocolate. They have discovered a new passion that changes their lives for the better.

I am always delighted to meet them later – for I feel quite evangelical about spreading the word about chocolate. I love to discover that I have given someone else the chance to experience the enormous pleasure I derive from chocolate.

Desert island chocolates

When I ask people *why* they like certain kinds of chocolate, their answers can be very revealing. Often a particular chocolate evokes special memories. It may be the first bar you ever tasted, or one you regularly shared with a brother or sister, bringing back warm feelings of love and connectedness. Taste (and, more importantly, smell, which makes up ninety per cent of what we taste) is powerfully linked with our unconscious mind, and the memories it revives can be quite amazing. To get to know chocolate, you need to understand your relationship with chocolate: what you like to eat, and why.

With this in mind, I love to get people to think about the different types of chocolate they would take with them if they were abandoned, Crusoe-style, on a desert island. What goes into *your* desert island suitcase?

Your list might contain anything from Cadbury Buttons (first encountered in a birthday party bag) to Galaxy – which you still indulge in when you need sustenance to get through a difficult project at work. Perhaps you've already discovered the intense pleasure of good-quality 70% dark chocolate, or the rich savour of nutty filled chocolates.

You may already have noticed that, when you take the time to taste chocolate, almost 'listening' to what each bar has to tell you, you learn that there is a lot more to it than 'milk' or 'plain'. Even 70% chocolate varies enormously. Once you start to notice these often very subtle differences, you are on your way to developing your own list of favourites or your 'survival kit' chocolates, and developing your palate as a connoisseur.

As an exercise, why not record your desert island list now? Can you think of ten different bars you'd take with you? When you've finished reading this book, go back to this list, and see whether it's changed.

In my survival kit...

People are forever asking me about my own favourite chocolate, as if I think that one bar alone is superior to all others. In fact, I always tell people that no individual's taste in chocolate is better or worse than anyone else's. My 'survival kit', or the list of chocolates that I love and can't do without, won't necessarily suit your tastes – and may not even fit mine in a few months' time.

As I have been a dedicated choco-explorer for many years, my kit is big and filled with bars you may not have come across, some of them not even sold over the counter yet. Column 2 of the chart on page 33 will give you an indication of some of the chocolates I return to again and again.

I keep a wide range of chocolates to match my different moods – and I actually couldn't choose one above all others! At any given time I'll have at least 20 different bars at home, all permanently opened and properly sealed to keep each future bite at its best. Although I would not have a bite from each one of the bars every day, there is not a week that passes without a reunion with each one.

But what matters is *your* taste – what special significance a certain chocolate holds for *you*. As you gradually try more and more of the bars mentioned in this book, some will resonate more than others. You'll find that a bar you try once and don't like suddenly hits you with a zing when you taste it again – perhaps you were just in the wrong mood for it the first time around. The more you learn, and the more you taste, and as you slowly build up your own 'survival kit', you will become able to match bar with mood, or clearly recognise when you hunger for a ganache (a chocolate filled with chocolate and cream), a nibble of Toblerone, or a few squares of something dark and challenging.

Your chocolate profile: step 3

To make the most of your discoveries, try to make notes about each new chocolate you encounter and how it made you feel. This will form the beginning of your own chocolate database.

- What did you feel when you put it in your mouth?

- How long did the flavours take to develop?

- What was your mood before you ate it? Were you happy and celebrating, or down and in need of comfort?

- What special significance (if any) did that new chocolate bring to your life that day?

The next time you taste the same chocolate, check back and see if you still feel the same way about it. This can be a very revealing exercise, because your palate will be developing without your realising it. For example, people who think they have learned something amazing when they discover a famous name in organic chocolate may later find that this chocolate gives them the kind of sweet aftertaste and astringency in the mouth and the throat that they get from a much cheaper product. There's more about developing your chocolate database in Chapter 4.

Is your palate primed?

'Tell me what you eat, and I will tell you what you are,' said the nineteenth-century French gourmand Brillat-Savarin. This holds for chocolate, too.

As you proceed through this book you will be monitoring changes in the way you taste and appreciate chocolate. Your palate may already have been primed by a growing appreciation of other foods.

- Do you buy fine cheeses from the delicatessen or do you prefer the ease of vacuum-packed slices from the supermarket?

- Do you ever buy olive oil or tea from specialised shops, trying different origins or blends to discover their range?

- Do you pop into the coffee shop closest to you, or do you walk the extra block to a café that makes wonderful coffee?

- Do you avoid sandwiches made with white sliced bread?

- Do you prefer a full-fat yogurt over a low-fat one?

Most of us have certain expectations about food. You might worry that as you grow more discerning about what you eat, you are becoming a food snob. But I prefer to put it this way: you are discovering not only what you *really* like, but also the great pleasure that fine food can bring.

As a born chocoholic, I could never resist trying any new bar of chocolate I came across – and when I moved to Paris in my teens, I encountered enough new bars of chocolate to keep me going for months. My shopping expeditions yielded nuances of flavour I had never encountered before, and, with these discoveries, I started to develop a chocolate database where I listed my tasting notes and comparisons between different chocolates of the same cocoa percentage or country of origin.

Maybe this sounds like hard work, but believe me, it's not. It's all about pleasure – listening to your body, tasting new tastes, storing the memory of them. Brillat-Savarin wrote in 1826: 'The discovery of a new dish brings more to human happiness than the discovery of a star.' Except I substitute 'chocolate' for 'dish', of course!

Join the club!

Even if you relish buying different chocolate bars, and making notes on them, you may find this quite a solitary pastime. And although I actually recommend solitary chocolate sessions as a way of developing your palate (see Chapter 4), chocolate is also very much for sharing – and sharing with another impassioned soul is a way of learning. Just think of the number of times you have learned something new from chatting to a friend. You inevitably come away with a new bit of gossip, or a different perspective on an event in the news.

Coming together with a group of like-minded people is always a rich experience. Join a specialist chocolate club, and you will also learn who's making what, why it's deemed special, and where you can find it. You will get the opportunity to share your views on each chocolate, helping to further develop your database of information.

I have sometimes invited a curious friend to one of those meetings. Very soon they start laughing, finding it hilarious to see a diverse group of people discussing chocolate in the serious tones usually reserved for European art-house films or prize-winning literature. Well, to an outsider, maybe it does seem like madness! But it can be a life-changing experience. My own discovery of the Chocolate Society in 1991, when I was a student and living in London, had a dramatic influence on my development as a chocolate connoisseur.

I was visiting the chocolate shop Rococco on King's Road in London – an amazing Aladdin's cave of treasures – for the first time. In among the foil-covered chocolate sardines, parrots and rabbits for Easter, I saw a notice on the counter inviting customers to join the Chocolate Society. The leaflet read:

Chocolate not candy

The Chocolate Society was formed four years ago by three dedicated chocolate enthusiasts. One of the Society's first priorities is to draw attention to the difference between the complex delicacy the world's greatest cooks and gourmets recognise as chocolate, and the low grade, cloying confection which the British consume by the ton every week.

The principle ingredient of commercial chocolate bars and bonbons is not cocoa (on average a meagre 20% by volume) but sugar, saturated vegetable fat and powdered milk. These dietary villains are responsible for chocolate's undeserved reputation as a fattening, tooth-rotting, addictive indulgence.

True chocolate is a far purer, healthier product. A single square of Guanaja Noire (made by French manufacturers Valrhona, near Lyon) for example, contains 70% cocoa solids but only a tenth of the sugar of the typical so-called chocolate bar.

Strong words you may think, but if you are one of the growing band of chocolate enthusiasts who takes their chocolate seriously then why not become a friend of the Chocolate Society?

You will be in good company

The Chocolate Society is dedicated to elevating chocolate to its rightful status as one of the world's gourmet delights.

Fine chocolate, painstakingly produced from natural ingredients, is every bit as sophisticated as a great claret or single malt whisky. Each variety has its own distinctive character, aroma and flavour. Just like coffee, varying the origin, type and blend of cocoa bean opens an endless range of subtlety to the palate.

This couldn't have described my own beliefs and mission more accurately. I was overjoyed – and determined to become a member, even though the joining fee represented a week and a half of my student income at the time.

Through the Chocolate Society, my fixed ideas about chocolate were challenged and I learned to open up to new opinions – crucial if you really want to become a connoisseur. For example, through a chocolate tasting session hosted by the society, I met the Parisian chocolatier Robert Linxe, founder of La Maison du Chocolat. At the time I was one of those people I now come across all the time – the band of chocolate lovers who proudly claim they 'only eat dark chocolate'.

When Linxe offered me one of his chocolates, I proudly asked if it could be a dark one. He smiled and offered me a plain milk ganache, saying '*Goutez moi ça*' ('Taste this for me'). In front of *the* master of chocolate at that time, I swallowed my pride – and the chocolate, which turned out to be exceedingly good. From that day I have made it my policy to explain that I would rather eat a good milk chocolate than a bad dark one. And, if someone says they only like dark chocolate, I know they have not yet seen 'the light'.

The Chocolate Society still exists, with a shop in London and a website (www.chocolate.co.uk). And, these days, as well as having access to gourmet chocolate events and mail order shopping (a great way to get your hands on those chocolates that have not yet reached your part of the world), new members are sent a hamper full of chocolate goodies.

There's also a new UK club on the way: the Academy of Chocolate, which will offer chocolate awards and guidance about quality chocolate.

Another great site, dedicated to 'chocolate connoisseurs', is www.seventypercent.com, which sells itself as being interested in 'the pure stuff – chocolate bars – rather than products that are flavoured with chocolate or made with it, such as truffles or bonbons' (words that are music to my ears!). The Seventy Per Cent Club has a very good range of quality chocolate available by mail order, and, despite its name, you will find a wide range of milk chocolate as well as dark.

SHOPPING FOR CHOCOLATES

You will probably find as you read through these pages that you are encountering the names of many chocolates you have never seen in the shops. To find them, first search any delicatessens and fancy department store food halls near you. And if your search doesn't turn up all the brands you've read about, try the internet. There are many chocolate societies and chocolate suppliers who deliver all over the world – and many of my favourite chocolate makers also have their own websites. See Resources, pages 210–11 for some starting points.

And finally...

My father once asked what I would do if I ever became allergic to chocolate. His question stopped me in my tracks. From my scientific studies (I am a qualified agronomist) I knew it was possible to become allergic to practically anything at any time in one's life. But the thought of becoming allergic to chocolate was horrific. Then I realised I knew exactly what I would do. 'I would find another passion,' I told him.

Meanwhile, and thankfully, I'm not allergic to this intensely delicious substance. And once you have started to discover how very wonderful chocolate can be, you will, I am sure, be just as drawn to the taste of real chocolate – even though finding it won't always be easy. But if it was, we wouldn't need our desert island survival kits. We would know that we could walk into any chocolate shop and find the real thing.

Just why this should be the case is to do with the way that 95 per cent of the world's chocolate is manufactured. In the next chapter, I will take you through this long and complicated manufacturing process and help you to understand what it really takes to make good chocolate – and you'll begin to find it easier to distinguish the good from the bad.

CHAPTER 3

Bean to bar

*I*F I HAD MY WAY, chocolate bars (but only the very best, of course!) would grow on cocoa trees. Instead, what we have is a very ugly-looking fruit whose content has to go through a long and complex chain of events before it remotely resembles chocolate.

The good news is that, with human intervention, every stage of this process is an opportunity to maximise the quality of the chocolate and create a better bar.

The bad news is that quality is very often compromised in deference to profit. And if consumers seem to like the taste of the cheapened product, so much the better for the manufacturers!

Nowadays, the closest you can get to a chocolate factory tour is a *virtual* tour – in which trade secrets are firmly kept as trade secrets. I'm not going to show you how Cadbury, Hershey, or any other manufacturer makes chocolate, but in this chapter I will take you on my own virtual tour of the chocolate chain. And it begins at the very beginning, with the cocoa tree.

Tree of the tropics

Although you may fantasise about owning and nurturing one, the cocoa tree (*Theobroma cacao*) is fragile and fussy, and simply won't survive in an ordinary garden or conservatory outside the tropics. (You can visit one in the Palm House at London's Kew Gardens, however, and if you live near another botanical garden or a university offering tropical agronomy courses, look for one there.)

So what makes this precious little tree tick? Here's the lowdown:

- It grows only in tropical regions within the latitudes of 20° South and 20° North of the equator, where it is dependent on a year-round temperature of 70°F to 77°F (my ideal, too!). If you look at the map on page 53 you will see that the chocolate-producing countries form a belt around the equator.

- It is usually surrounded by other plants that provide shade (banana trees and leguminous trees). This is crucial when the tree is young, as it only needs to get 50 per cent of available light.

- It grows better between 1/4 mile and 3/4 mile above sea level, and requires at least 65–70 per cent humidity year-round.

- After three years, a typical tree measures 13–16 ft and at ten years it measures up to 26 ft.

The cocoa-producing regions

You will notice throughout this book that I often name the region where the beans used to make your bar of chocolate came from. Over a hundred years ago, it was possible – as it is now – to buy a 'single-estate' bar, made from beans from one specific region. In 1902, Bonnat did just this (his bars came from regions in Venezuela and Madagascar). Yet at that time, cocoa percentage was more important to chocolate-lovers than the origin.

Now, the origin of the cocoa beans used to make a bar is crucial information for the chocolate connoisseur. This is because the origin of the beans will dramatically affect the quality of the chocolate made from them. The well-established tradition in the wine world of indicating the region of the grape's provenance is becoming a growing trend in chocolate labelling. 'Single-estate' or 'single-origin' bar indicates that the cocoa beans used to produce a choco-late bar are from one region of a country (like 'Bordeaux' on a wine label). 'Plantation bar', or the specific name of a plantation (such as Michel Cluizel's *Concepcion* plantation in Venezuela), indicates that the chocolate comes from a particular plantation of a few acres, reowned for the quality of its beans – the equivalent of a *domaine* for wines. If you go to the most upmarket delis or department store food halls you will probably be able to find a few brands which already label their bars in this way.

The first wild cocoa trees are thought to have come from the Brazilian Amazon (though cocoa detectives have recently discovered DNA suggesting a separate line of trees originat-ing in Venezuela), but they were first cultivated in Mexico and its neighbouring countries, and it's from here that they gradually spread to other continents. The Latin American beans came from the Criollo tree – the most fragrant, but also the most fragile, as we've seen.

Colonialism had a lot to do with the spread of the cocoa bean, as demands 'back home' for chocolate increased from 1650 onward, and plantations were started up in tropical colonies.

The map on page 53 shows the current growing regions.

WHERE IN THE WORLD? ...

Ivory Coast and Ghana: Forastero beans reached Africa in 1822, and by 1921 Africa had replaced the Americas as the major cocoa-producing continent. Today Ivory Coast and Ghana share seventy per cent of world production – all Forasteros.

Indonesia: Cocoa from Mexico was introduced to Indonesia in 1515 by the Spanish, but commercial and intense exploitation only started in the 1970s. Most Indonesian cocoa is acidic and poor quality; only Java has very fine cocoa.

Brazil: Brazil was the world's second biggest cocoa producer until 1986, when disease decimated most of the trees. The country now produces only four per cent of the world's cocoa, and has to import beans to satisfy internal demand.

Mexico: The birthplace of manufactured cocoa, Mexico now produces mainly lower-quality cocoa. Interestingly, a few rare, fragrant Criollo trees grow wild in the jungle of Chiapas in the south. Attempts are underway to revive this precious species.

Venezuela: The country became a major cocoa producer at the beginning of the seventeenth century. But recession and cyclone damage in the early 1930s conspired to change all that and now Venezuela has just 0.5 per cent of the cocoa market. However, it is one of the world's top three countries in terms of quality. Venezuela is a special case as it is likely to be the first country in the world where specific bean-growing regions will be strictly defined and labelling regulated – thus protecting the special high-quality regional beans against copycats and false marketing. See page 134 for more details.

Equador: The country was the world's number one cocoa producer in 1850. Today, it has three per cent of world production and is the world's eighth biggest producer. Equadorian cocoa is more interesting than anything produced in Africa, but I don't yet rate it very highly.

Madagascar: The country produces less than 0.5 per cent of world production, but most are fine-quality cocoa beans.

Jamaica: Jamaica also grows less than 0.5 per cent of the world's cocoa, and the beans are often poor quality or poorly fermented.

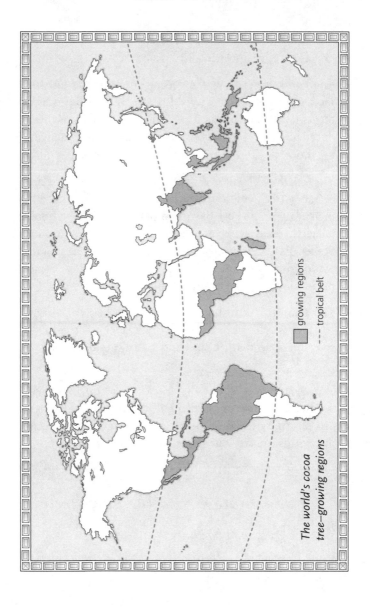

growing regions
--- tropical belt

The world's cocoa
tree-growing regions

The varieties

There are three main varieties of cocoa tree:

- **The Forastero**. This is the most common, and also the most robust and highest-yielding. Sadly, it also produces the least aromatic beans. This is the tree Europeans introduced into their plantations in the colonies when demand for chocolate grew in the early twentieth century.

- **The Criollo**. This variety is everything the Forastero is not. A fragile tree, with a very small yield, it is considered by many to give the best-flavoured bean. Today most books tell us that two to five per cent of cocoa trees are Criollos. Specialists in agronomy think less than one per cent of the world production is Criollo. Modern-day Criollos are not pure Criollo, but a Criollo/Trinitario hybrid.

- **The Trinitario** is descended from a cross between Criollo and Forastero. This tree has hybrid characteristics – robustness, aromatic beans, and a fairly good yield.

You may also hear about the Nacional, a fourth variety, which was once cultivated in Equador until plantations were wiped out by Witch Broom disease, a form of tree cancer. Only hybrids (of Trinitario and Nacional) remain.

The resistable rise of the Forastero

What makes good chocolate?

The fine, fragrant beans from Criollo or good Trinitario trees are the best starting point.

What makes bad chocolate?

Poor-quality beans from uninteresting Forastero trees.

Yet 85 per cent of the world's chocolate today originates from Forastero trees. So what went wrong?

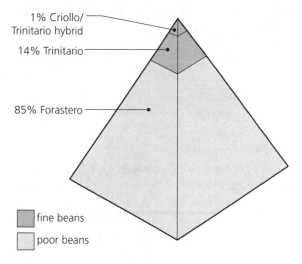

1% Criollo/
Trinitario hybrid

14% Trinitario

85% Forastero

fine beans
poor beans

Quality pyramid: world production of cocoa beans

In the nineteenth century, Criollo or Trinitario trees would only have been replaced with hardier varieties if disease or other natural disaster had destroyed the plantation. But in the early twentieth century, human greed for profits pushed many producing countries to destroy the Criollo trees and replace them with stronger and more productive Forasteros. I call it chococide – the genocide of good cocoa trees.

Why was this? The reason is that beans are sold at the same price per kilo, whatever their quality. And the vast majority of plantations are, in reality, small farms less than five hectares in size. If you were one of these small farmers, struggling to make ends meet and get enough money to buy basic necessities, and you could produce twice the quantity of beans by swapping your Criollo or Trinitario trees for Forasteros, you would have to be mad, suicidal or a masochist not to do so. Survival comes first. And most of the time producers do not even know that the weaker tree produces the more aromatic beans.

It takes seven years for a cocoa seedling to grow into a tree that is mature enough to produce pods. So, from the very start of the process, you can see why the poor farmers (for most are very poor) are reluctant to waste valuable time raising a fragile, aromatic tree when a robust but not so fragrant variety will thrive with ease.

But there is good news. This depressing situation is being turned around. The chocolate company Domori from Italy started replanting true Criollos in 1997 (using seeds from a gene bank in Trinidad). And international agronomy research centres such as the CIRAD (which has a programme to revive the Nacional tree in Ecuador and the Criollo in Madagascar) are following in their footsteps. In the next few years, we connoisseurs will experience unique aromas in chocolate that it is unlikely anyone has experienced in the last 100 years.

How it all begins: raw material

The pod

Cocoa trees, regardless of their variety, produce fruit all year round, although there are two main harvests in May and November. If you get a chance to see a tree, its mixture of blossom and pods at different stages of development is quite stunning. The cocoa pod grows straight out of the trunk, and I remember that the first time I saw them I thought the tree was diseased, with its gnarled and bulbous protrusions.

Cocoa pods growing on a tree

But the more familiar I became with the trees, the more I learned to love this characteristic. I am now fascinated by the variety of colours and hues of the different pods – golden yellow, orange, red, burgundy. After one plantation trip to Haiti, I took a lot back home hoping to build a collection, but they rotted. Since then I learned to gently dry them out at home on the radiator, but they shrink, become wrinkled and their wonderful colour fades.

Angoleto
Pods are long and ridged with wide shoulders and little or no bottleneck. The tip is usually somewhat pointed but not curved.

Cundeamor
Pods are long, warty, deeply ridged and furrowed, with either a pronounced bottleneck, or a suggestion of one, and a pointed tip which is sometimes curved.

Amelonado
Pods have melonlike shape, shallow ridges and furrows and tip is rounded, rather than pointed, with faint hint of a bottleneck. The skin is thick, and usually smooth with occasional wartiness.

Calabacillo
Pods are shaped like a small pumpkin and are round or oval with thick and very smooth skin. They have almost no ridges or furrows and no suggestion of tip or bottleneck. (Its colour is grass green changing to deep yellow as it matures.)

Four types of shape of cocoa pod (no link with genetics)

The bean

As soon as the pods are ripe enough, they are cut from the tree with a machete. They grow so close to the trunk that this is a delicate operation – the trunk can be easily damaged and is vulnerable to disease, so harvesting with machines will never be possible. The pods are then piled together for a group of workers to open by hand.

Split pod revealing cocoa beans

Within the pod, the beans lie wrapped in a thick protective coating of white mucilage, looking a bit like a bunch of grapes covered in soggy cotton wool. All this is emptied into large baskets or containers. The mucilage is juicy and fresh, with delicate aromas that vary from one tree to another. The flavour is honeyish, with a faint vanilla aftertaste, and plantation workers and their children love to suck this, and spit out the bitter beans.

RIPENESS IS ALL

What makes good chocolate?
Juicy ripe pods, from fine trees.

What makes bad chocolate?
Pods that have not been allowed to ripen fully, and have been cut off too soon.

This happens because poor farmers are living hand to mouth and want their bean cash as soon as they can get it.

First-stage processing

Fermentation and flavour

The mucilage needs to be removed from the beans before processing, so, most commonly, layers of fruity pulp are put in wooden boxes with holes at the bottom (which act like a colander), and covered with banana tree leaves which contain bacteria that enhance the fermentation process, liquefying the mucilage so it can drain away, leaving the beans.

This process also brings out the precursors of the aromas that the resulting chocolate will have – a crucial factor if you care about quality and full flavours.

COCOA LIQUEURS

The drained liquid may occasionally be reserved and used for cocoa liqueur that keeps all the aromas of the mucilage, tasting more like honey and vanilla than chocolate. When buying cocoa liqueurs, check whether they're made from the bean, or from the mucilage; the latter is relatively rare.

By the book, fermentation should take five to seven days, although Criollo beans are faster to ferment and may be ready in three to four days. These lengths of time are needed to give the cocoa beans' aromas the best chance of developing. Unfortunately, co-operatives, like the small farmers who supply them, are often hungry for cash, and buyers from the big companies are not very interested in aroma. To all parties, there may seem little point in wasting precious time on fermentation when they can get the transaction over as soon as the beans have been sufficiently drained.

Down at the co-op...

Most farmers take their baskets of mucilage to their nearest co-operative, very often a neat little two-roomed house built with a grant from the cocoa programme of an international agency. Posters on the walls show pictures of different beans cut lengthwise so the farmer can see what 'faults' the co-operative wants to prevent ending up in the bags they will sell on to exporters or international companies. Fifty of each farmer's beans are placed on a flat metallic dish, with one hole for each bean. They are then cut in two, lengthwise, with a guillotine or knife and checked against the wall charts.

As we've seen, most co-operatives are not looking for quality, as they receive the same price regardless of whether the tree is a Criollo or a Forastero, or whether the pod is ripe or distinctly unripe. They are looking for size (100–150 beans 5 oz), a low humidity level (below six per cent), and minimal faults. Often, quality control is carried out by a group of women sitting on the floor and sorting the beans by their appearance (never the taste!). And they are allowed to take the 'bad' beans home to make chocolate drinks. Is this the best way to guarantee the quality of the beans that will end up in our favourite chocolate bars? I'll leave that up to your imagination!

Drying

Once the beans are drained of mucilage, the next step is to dry them to the point where they contain less than six to eight per cent moisture. This will prevent them from going mouldy when shipped, and allows them to be stored for four to five years without going off – although most factories store only what they need for three weeks of grinding.

Some farmers dry their own beans and sell them on themselves, rather than taking them to a co-operative. In these instances, the farmer may simply spread his beans onto a side-street and let the sun do the work of drying: the cement of the street may be the only hot, dry surface to which he has access. But, while it is better than the crude earthy floor of a typical farmhouse at keeping moisture away from the beans, the street leaves the produce open to crushing by cars or children at play, theft, and dirt.

The alternative is to take the beans to a co-operative, most of which have special drying areas. These are either basic cemented outdoor areas, where the beans can dry hygienically in the sun by day (but are brought in overnight to prevent the dew getting to them); or dedicated drying rooms where the beans are laid out on racks suspended about a metre above huge pipes containing hot air. The way that cocoa beans are dried can greatly affect the flavour of the chocolate. The aim should be to dry the beans slowly, softly caressing them rather than blasting them with the equivalent of a hair-dryer, which is sadly what happens in many drying rooms.

THE ART OF DRYING

Steve de Vries, one of the passionate chocolatiers who I believe is leading the chocolate revolution, has been experimenting with the drying of beans. He gave me two chocolates to sample – one made with beans that had been slowly and tenderly 'caressed' dry by the sun at its less-intense times (from 5 am to 10 am and from 5 pm until nightfall), the other made from identical beans which were sun-dried conventionally, in well-monitored drying rooms.

The difference in taste was spectacular. A fingernail-sized morsel just .10cm thick of the specially dried chocolate was packed with fresh aromas of plums and tropical fruit that lasted a good five minutes. In the other sample I detected the same fruity aromas, but they were less intense, less clean, and swimming in the earthy, rustic aromas I associate with a typical Equadorian chocolate. The first sample was purity, elegance – in taste terms, a white cloud with angels dancing on it. The 'sun-bed', as I call the other one, was a beautiful orchid lost in the middle of a dirty, noisy city.

Off to the Factory

After drying, the beans are put in 130 lb jute bags and sprayed with chemicals to prevent damage from weevils, vermin or bugs. They are then sent on the long journey to the countries where they will be processed.

Roasting and shelling

To bring out the chocolate flavour and colours the beans are roasted. The temperature, time and degree of moisture involved in roasting depends on the type of beans being used and the type of chocolate being made. Thus, when the chocolate is made with a different blend of beans, beans are roasted separately and mixed afterwards

A winnowing machine is used to remove the shells from the beans to leave what are known as the cocoa nibs – peeled beans transformed into chunks.

Many companies now sell pure cocoa nibs. Nibs, chopped into small chunks, even turn up in chocolate bars. The chocolate company Weiss kicked this fashion off in 1994 with its Noir aux Eclats de Fèves (dark chocolate with fragments of cocoa beans).

If you get the chance to taste a nib, I recommend you do so – if only for the shock it will give you. You may well expect the roundness and sweetness of chocolate, but you won't find it. It's an extreme experience ... and one that will leave you fully understanding why Europeans found the unsweetened Aztec version of hot chocolate so unpalatable.

It is only this year that I have begun to deeply enjoy eating nibs. I should say that these were very special, made from fine-quality beans fermented and dried with the utmost care. There are, I discovered, nibs and nibs. Most of the ones available at the moment are what you might politely call an acquired taste – and the fact that they can be transformed into such an exquisite concoction is due to the added vanilla and sugar, not the beans.

This is summed up perfectly in a quote from the French food writer James de Coquet: '*Il faut avoir gouté aux fèves de cacao pour mesurer toute la somme de génie que l'homme peut metre au service de son appétit de volupté.*' In other words, what a genius man can be when he's motivated by his hunger for pleasure!

Cocoa liquor, cocoa butter and cocoa presscake

At the factory, the nibs are then milled to create cocoa liquor (peeled and ground cocoa beans). This paste has the consistency of peanut butter and is at last starting to smell something like chocolate. The cocoa liquor is pressed to extract the cocoa butter, leaving a solid matter called cocoa presscake. The machines used by the big companies to do this are based on the one invented by the nineteenth-century Dutch chemist, Van Houten. The machines eject the watery, lemon-yellow melted cocoa butter and leave a cocoa presscake about 2 in thick and 1 foot in diameter.

Alternatives for fine or cheap chocolate

The process now takes two different directions:

- A. The cocoa butter is added to the cocoa liquor in the production of fine chocolate.

- B. Unfortunately, most cheap chocolate is made with a combination of cocoa powder (made from pulverised cocoa presscake) and vegetable fats, which are a much cheaper substitute for cocoa butter.

> Before 2003, EU rulings allowed manufacturers in Britain and the Netherlands to add up to 5 per cent vegetable fats without declaring it on the label, and it was this which led EEC ministers in 1985 to suggest that British chocolate should be called 'vegelate' rather than chocolate! Ironically, in 2003 this was widened to include all EU countries, and now 'vegelate' is made throughout Europe.

The next steps

Other ingredients such as sugar, milk, vanilla, and emulsifying agents such as lecithin, are added and mixed. The mixture then undergoes a refining process by travelling through a series of rollers until a smooth paste is formed. This improves the texture.

Conching

The paste is transferred to the conche, a machine which kneads and smooths the chocolate mixture for up to three days at a temperature between 140°F to 167°F, depending on the company. Some companies, such as Amedei, still use conches based on the original Lindt design, but the modern conches used by the majority of companies are very different and usually totally electronically managed.

The speed, duration and temperature of the conching affect the flavour. Conching also improves the texture, and allows any acidity to evaporate.

If you have ever read Roald Dahl's story *Charlie and the Chocolate Factory*, you will recall that the smell on approaching a chocolate factory can make you nauseated – in fact, a lot of people stop eating chocolate after two days of working in a chocolate factory. The reason is that the acetic fumes from the conching are the same as those in vinegar.

THE CONCH CONNECTION

What makes good chocolate?
Long conching. Conching should take at least two to three days, according to Lindt's instructions. I recently tasted chocolate at Amedei's factory that had been conched for three hours, nine hours, two days and three days respectively. The improvement with time was clear (although it would also be possible to over-conch a chocolate).

What makes bad chocolate?
Inadequate conching, which is done to cut costs. You can only be suspicious when a big company prides itself on conching for just five hours instead of the two to three days applied by Amedei, Valrhona, Domori, Pralus, Scharffen Berger and others. Yet at a major chocolate symposium in 2003, one expert presented his 'zero conching' theory. Lindt must have been turning in his grave!

Tempering

After conching, the chocolate mixture is 140°F to 167°F and needs to be cooled to around 104°F to allow stable crystallisation of the cocoa butter. Cocoa butter is basically made of six types of crystals which melt at different temperatures. By tempering, cocoa butter goes through a number of variations of temperatures and an inner grid of stable crystals is formed. The process produces a chocolate that is shiny and smooth, with a homogenous and silky texture. The melted chocolate eventually comes out of a tap – which must be every chocoholic's dream!

There's a lovely story about an American pastry teacher on a guided tour of the El Rey factory, near Caracas, Venezuela, who asked if she could swim in their tempering machine. The company explained that, unfortunately, this would not be possible for hygiene reasons. But they were able to accommodate her by providing a private room in which she could climb into a hot tub filled with melted chocolate. It took her two hours to wash it all off!

What makes good chocolate?
Careful tempering. To temper chocolate, you heat and melt it (around 104°F) and then cool it down very quickly, as the most stable of the six fat crystals in cocoa butter, used to prompt the crystallisation of the others, crystallises at the lower temperature. This is the reason why chocolatiers always work with chocolate on a marble slab.

What makes bad chocolate?
Careless tempering. When tempering isn't properly carried out the result is a grainy, crunchy chocolate with no shine, and possibly a grey or white film on the surface called 'bloom' (which is the fat coming to the top). If you have ever tasted a chocolate bar that crunches with crystals or has a powdery texture, it is because something went wrong with the tempering process.

Moulding

After tempering, the 90°F liquid chocolate is stored as a liquid for later use (see 'couverture', pages 118–20) or poured into moulds and placed in a cooling tunnel. The bars are then removed from the moulds and wrapped – usually by machines. After a very long and complex chain of chemical and physical reactions, the chocolate bar is ready to bring more pleasure to our life.

Storing up pleasure

Once they've left the factory, chocolate bars have an 18-month shelf life. Filled chocolates last just three weeks (unless they're packed with alcohol, sugar and artificial preservatives). Proper storage will keep chocolate in top condition within those time limits – but how do you manage it once you've got the chocolate safely home?

When I lived and worked in Jamaica as an agronomist, chocolate was hard to come by in the shops (again, it's a case of the producing country rarely getting to enjoy the product it supplies), and I had to find a way of storing the huge supplies of chocolate I brought into the country. I still rely on this storage system today, and recommend it to anyone wanting to keep good chocolate for a long period – especially if you rarely get the opportunity to stock up on supplies.

In warm climates (above 80°F–86°F), store your bars in the fridge (never freeze them as you will kill their texture). Wrap them safely in a food bag (squeezing out all the air before you close it) to prevent them from becoming contaminated with the humidity and smells of the other food in the fridge. When you remove the bars, leave them in the bag until they reach room temperature. Then wrap them in a paper towel to absorb any condensation and prevent this from moistening and defiling the chocolate. They will be ready to eat when they have reached room temperature – normally within 20 minutes.

Only filled chocolates can be stored in a freezer (for up to six months). Package them in the same way as the bars, but plan 24 hours ahead before eating them. To defrost them, place them, still bagged, in the fridge for 24 hours, then remove and leave at room temperature for half an hour in a hot country or two hours in a cooler country (or in the evening in a hot country). Then open the bag, wrap the chocolates in a piece of paper towel (to absorb the condensation) and leave for another 10 to 15 minutes to get them to room temperature before serving.

If you are like me and like to eat three different types of filled chocolates every day, whatever your rations, you need to avoid storing each type separately. Instead, prepare daily assortments in separate bags, mini survival kits. If you can afford it, and want to store for a long time (for example, if you live far from a good supplier), invest in a machine for vacuum packing, and use this prior to refrigerating or freezing your supplies. Even better, store them in a wine fridge.

DIY chocolate

If you already make your own bread, ice cream and jam, if you love the control you get from making anything from scratch, and, if you are a true chocophile, it may have crossed your mind that maybe, just maybe, you could also make your own chocolate.

For you to produce your own chocolate from the bean, you would need to invest around $90,000 in machinery (and that's secondhand!). But, on a very small scale, you *can* make it happen at home.

If you need inspiration, look up stories about the child prodigy Amy Singh, who at 11, was exhibiting her own 56% blend of chocolate at international chocolate shows, which she had made herself with Venezuelan Trinitario beans. Amy uses two vegetable steamer baskets wired together, attached to the rotisserie rod of an outdoor grill for roasting. After husking and winnowing the beans, she grinds them in a coffee mill, then puts them through a pasta machine to refine them with powdered sugar and vanilla bean seeds. After a couple of passes through the pasta machine, the mixture is put into another type of pasta machine for conching. The heat source is a standard lamp.

Using these tools, made from household appliances, she has apparently been able to reduce her chocolate to particles of around 20 microns in size – well below what can be felt on the tongue – and in line with many of the best chocolates in the world that aim for 16 microns.

Even as a choco-connoisseur, I wouldn't aspire to such a thing. But, a few years ago, I had the privilege of making chocolate with Claudio Corallo – a truly passionate, perfectionist chocologist, and the man behind a special 'plantation' chocolate bar by the French company Pralus. Claudio and his family own a small cocoa plantation in São Tomé e Príncipe. They now have a small co-operative factory for their chocolate production. But at that time they made chocolate at home in their kitchen – to entertain the children and boost their morale and love for the product they are manufacturing. So, one day, as I was nearing the end of my stay, I asked them to show me how they did it.

We roasted some beans in the oven, peeled them by hand, carefully removing the acrid stem at the centre of each one, and then ground them by hand with some sugar in an old-fashioned coffee mill. The friction of milling causes the cocoa butter (50–55 per cent of the bean's content) to melt, and, out of the mill's spout came squidgy peanut butter–textured cocoa mass. Using our hands, we moulded this into bars. But these were nothing like the chocolate bars most consumers know.

The developed-country version is, as we've seen, highly processed to achieve its smooth texture – a process which Corallo says kills chocolate. He calls mass-market chocolate 'the corpse of real chocolate' because it has had all the life sucked out of it. The bars we made were grainy, with sugar crystals and crumbs from the nibs – far from perfect – but, for the connoisseur in search of the true taste of chocolate, this was closer to the real thing than anything you find in a typical supermarket. Today Corallo has developed a whole range of plain chocolates totally different from anything you can find in the supermarket.

Poor-quality chocolate is the equivalent of a ready-made meal, smothered in salt and sugar and artificial flavourings. People get used to that taste, and find it hard to enjoy real food when they are unaccustomed to it. The chocolate I made at

Claudio Corallo's had a somewhat crude consistency, some unpleasant smoky and cheesy notes, but its flavour was natural – not stifled by nasty additives. And of course there was the satisfaction of knowing we had made it ourselves!

And finally...

Three million tons of cocoa beans are processed worldwide every year, but ever since conching – still the most momentous improvement in chocolate bar production – took off, every step of the industrial development that has given us today's mass-market chocolate bar has taken us further and further away from the true taste of chocolate.

What drives me and my fellow 'chocologists' is a mission to bring about the changes needed to give the whole world, not just a lucky elite, the true, pure chocolate we all deserve. We know it is possible – but at a price.

- Manufacturers have to be prepared to devote more TLC to their plantations – growing the more fragile but more fragrant species of cocoa trees.

- Co-operatives must be encouraged to ferment their beans adequately to entice the delicious aromas out of them.

- More care must be given to drying and conching.

Now that the world is waking up to the fact that chocolate can be as fine as the finest wine – and prices will reflect this more and more – some producing countries are realising what a jewel they possess in their cocoa trees. These countries will help to force the changes that will bring more of us the gourmet bars of chocolate that I will be showing you how to taste in the next chapter.

CHAPTER 4

·

Tasting, tasting…

*M*OST PEOPLE ENJOY eating chocolate. But only a few make a habit of 'tasting' it in the same way that wine is tasted for its subtle notes of woodiness, spice, fresh fruit and floral bouquets (yes, all these flavours can be found in good chocolate too!).

But time and patience can, I believe, enable anyone with the right determination to become a chocolate connoisseur. Even if chocolate is merely a comfort food for you now, or just a small after-dinner treat, there is no reason why you can't also start on a connoisseur's tasting regime, choosing a time of day when you can sample chocolate in a studious way. The idea may be completely new to you, but it will ultimately enhance the enjoyment you derive from chocolate as you start to discover its secret aromas.

You won't need to throw away your favourite bars. But you will need to establish a new routine for your 'chocolate work', as this is the only way to give yourself the time you'll need to explore the world of fine chocolate. And it is a different world altogether.

- Good chocolate contains flavours you are not used to associating with chocolate – for example, mushrooms, flowers, berries, liquorice and even leather.

- It is like a symphony with many different notes – some come and go, others linger. Flavours may come in bursts, one after the other – and the aftertaste can be something completely different from the initial taste. Generally, as with wine, you should be able to distinguish a clear beginning, middle and end.

- The taste (aromas, not sweetness) can linger for many minutes if the chocolate is of exceptional quality.

Once you discover the new kind of chocolate I'm talking about, there will be no going back. Moving on from sweet overprocessed chocolate is like giving up sugar in your tea, or cutting excess salt out of your diet. You will one day wonder why you ever liked it so much.

Learning to taste

If all of this sounds interesting, it may be time for you to move on to the next stage of tasting – trying chocolate in a more studious way.

To do this you will need to engage all five senses, but above all, you will have to work at developing your palate. You will also have to create exam-like conditions for your studies, and learn to tune into your body (it helps if you're used to doing this – perhaps through yoga or meditation, but it's not a prerequisite!). This will give you the confidence to trust your judgement on all matters chocolatey.

MUSHROOMS IN A WET FOREST?

I started tasting chocolate properly as a teenager but it took me years of hard work before people began to think of me as an expert. As I have already mentioned, I began by working, unpaid, in one of Paris's top patisseries, Ladurée. The interview with the head chocolatier Pierre Hermé (who now has his own bijou chocolate stores) was a humbling experience. In my application I had written that I believed I had 'a good palate', a point he was quick to challenge.

Soon after my arrival at 8.30 am, he pushed a pile of ten dark chocolate bars towards me, and one by one cut a tiny square from each one, and handed the first to me with the instruction, 'Tell me what you think!' The chocolates were a brand I had never encountered before, Pralus, and each bar was labelled with the name of an exotic country such as Venezuela, Equador, or Madagascar. All were 75 % cocoa.

I tasted the first one: 'A walk in the forest, a wet forest,' I said.

He put a square of the same chocolate into his own mouth, and added: '...with mushrooms on the ground!'

With the second, I tasted 'bread'. Pierre found 'bis-cottes!' (rusks).

And so we went on. At last – I'd found someone who spoke my language!

And the test? I had proven that I knew there was more to chocolate than simply dark or milk. But my

real success was understanding that ten dark chocolates with the same cocoa solid content could be
totally different from one another – and not only that,
but being able to translate into words what my body
was telling me about the flavour of each one. I used the
method that wine tasters do, of linking the tastes in
the chocolate to the environment around me. (See
page 87 for more about how to do this.)

If you enjoy dark chocolate, and pride yourself on
eating only those with 70% cocoa content or more, try
sampling different brands of fine chocolate of similar
cocoa percentages, from different plantations or
countries of origin – and see how much more than just
a dark chocolate taste you can detect in each one.

Your biggest hurdle may be your own self-
confidence. A lot of people find it difficult to form their
own opinions on anything because they are so used to
being led by what others think, or are worried their
opinion will seem stupid, or offensive to someone
who doesn't share it. Becoming a connoisseur does
take a degree of front. You have to be prepared to
accept that your own opinions are as valid as anyone
else's. And you also need to be prepared to revise your
view if you've misjudged something!

When I was in my late twenties, I formed my own chocolate
club, *L'Association Carrément Chocolat* (which, translated
literally, means the Fully/Squarely Chocolate Association), in
order to initiate others into the art of tasting chocolate.
Everyone who attended loved chocolate – but they had not

yet developed the ability to appreciate it in the way that they would a fine wine.

But chocolate can give as much pleasure (far more in my case!) as a wine whose alcoholic content is lost in the alchemy of wondrous aromas (and bad chocolate is just as ghastly as a wine in which all flavour is drowned by the liquor). When you learn to taste chocolate properly you will discover that each chocolate has its own uniqueness that can add to your personal chocolate database – the store of information to which you will refer frequently as you become a chocolate connoisseur.

If you are familiar with wine tasting, you will find that the methodology for tasting chocolate is very similar. If chocolate is your initiation into the world of tasting, you may be about to learn that you have a hidden talent for detecting the symphony of flavours waiting to be discovered – not only in chocolate but in other food products too. I have personally tested apples, yogurts, cheeses, teas, coffees and spices using the same methodology, and it really is an eye-opener!

The five-sense test

To taste – be it chocolate, wine, tea, coffee or cheese – you need to engage all five senses. The wine critic Jancis Robinson explains this methodology very clearly and entertainingly in her book *How to Taste*, which I thoroughly recommend to anyone who wants to become an expert. But here I will cover the basics.

1. Use your eyes

Look at the piece of chocolate you are about to taste, evaluating its texture before you put it in your mouth. The surface should be smooth and shiny, indicating that the cocoa butter is properly crystallised (tempered). Do not be swayed by the colour. There are few rules about what colour is best, and the shade of chocolate colour is influenced by many factors such as bean type and roasting time as well as milk content.

2. Touch it

Is it soft or hard? Sticky, grainy, sandy or velvety? Crisp or crunchy? Getting to know the feel of a chocolate will help you recognise it again in the future. It will also help you to identify quality. The smoother the texture, the more unctuous it will be in the mouth. The finer the chocolate's particles, the greater the aromas you will find in it.

3. Listen to it

Even your ability to hear affects taste – and loss of hearing can give the impression that a food has a strange taste. Tuning in to the sound that your chocolate makes when you break it is another way of familiarising yourself with the product, and assessing its quality. Did it break easily? Neatly? Drily? A chocolate that snaps without too much effort is a sign that the balance between cocoa and butter is right. Dark chocolate snaps more easily than milk because, unlike milk chocolate, it contains no milk powder.

4. Smell it

Taste is ninety per cent smell. Our sensing equipment seems to pick up subtleties in aroma or vapour that we cannot detect in solids and liquids. You will have noticed that food is more tasteless when you have a cold and your nose is blocked up. You may even lose your appetite for it because there is nothing to savour.

The vapour given off by food or drink and warmed up in the mouth has two routes to the brain. When we sniff it, with the aim of taking in its odour, the vapour travels up our nose to the olfactory receptors at the top. When we are tasting, the same vapour takes a back route, from the back of the mouth, up what's called the retro-nasal passage, to the same sensory organ.

To test the affect that smell has on taste, try holding your nose and chewing a piece of flavoursome food. Then repeat the same exercise with your nose liberated.

THE ODOUR OF QUALITY

I have occasionally been invited to taste chocolate 'live' on TV. On one occasion I shocked the presenter by categorising the unwrapped 'mystery' chocolates as either 'cheap and poor quality' or 'interesting and probably expensive' before I had even put them in my mouth. 'But how do you know?' she asked. 'You haven't even tasted them!'

'No, but I smelled them,' I told her, thrilled at the thought that the thousands of people watching would now know how much you can learn from smelling a chocolate! Cheap chocolate is easily identified by its overpowering smell of vanilla and sugar, and good-quality chocolate is all about wondrous aromas – the woody, spicy and floral smells I've mentioned.

Our sense of smell is a bit like a memory bank. You know yourself how the smell of freshly cut grass may bring back memories of your childhood, how the scent of freshly shelled peas can take you back to your grandmother's kitchen in the summer, and how the smell of perfume or aftershave can remind you of the loved one who wears it. (Eau Sauvage always brings back thoughts of my father, for example.) It takes practice to describe a chocolate's 'nose', but we do so by relating aromas to those in our past experience. 'The more we penetrate odours,' observed the great twentieth-century perfumer and philosopher Edmond Roudnitska, 'the more they end up possessing us. They live within us, becoming an integral part of us, participating in a new function within us.'

The problem is that, in today's world, we are so bombarded by artificial smells that many of us have lost our database of natural scents. Sadly, when a lot of people smell a fine chocolate for the first time, they do not recognise it as chocolate. For them, chocolate should smell of sugar and vanilla! But practice makes perfect – to coin a cliché.

Good cocoa smells often remind us of natural products – fruit, flowers, woodlands or spice. A chocolate that smells smoky may have been carelessly dried. One that smells mouldy has been damaged in storage. You can build up your database of smells by using your nose whenever and wherever you can – not only when you are smelling chocolate.

Experience the scents of wet weather. If you're in the woods, smell the soil and the leaves. Breathe in the odour of a tree trunk. When you go to the market, take a sniff of each basket of mushrooms, herbs, fruit and flowers. Do all this and you will rediscover the potential of your sense of smell. We all have the ability, but many of us have forgotten it.

5. *Taste it*

When tasting a new chocolate, try just a small, fingernail-sized piece. Put it on your tongue and chew for a few seconds to break it into smaller chunks. Then stop and allow it to melt so that all flavours are released. Make sure the chocolate is spread all around your mouth – this way you'll taste the flavours most intensely.

Flavours

When the taste of a wonderful chocolate reverberates long after we have consumed the chocolate, that indicates our olfactory system is going into overdrive. Our taste buds play a relatively minor role, picking up only crude definitions: sweet, acid, salty and bitter.

When you start tasting truly good chocolate, you will find that its flavour can linger for many minutes. This is the best incentive I can think of to invest in an expensive bar. It may cost three times as much as your usual bar, but the pleasure you'll get from it is intense and long.

The flavour of chocolate comes from the combination of several of the basic tastes listed opposite. Sugar, and slightly acidic beans, can both act in the same way – in small quantities, they'll enhance the flavour but in larger quantites they drown it out. (Try a 99% bar once when you're feeling brave. Without the sugar, chocolate is a very different beast!) Fine chocolate has harmonious tastes – you'll need to concentrate to sense their presence. Look out in particular for bitterness, acidity and astringency. The first two are welcome, but astringency is a bad sign, often found in poor-quality chocolate. Next, I'll show you how to identify these tastes.

Sweetness

Sweetness is tasted at the tip of the tongue. My simple rule with sweetness is this: if you notice the sugar, if it annoys you slightly, there is too much of it in the bar. Excess sugar is used to disguise poor-quality or uninteresting beans, covering up the burnt, metallic or mouldy flavours you might otherwise taste.

sweet

Each time you taste a new chocolate, think about the sugar. Is it noticeable? Does it override the other flavours?

Bitterness, sourness and acidity

When I introduce novices to real chocolate, many use the word 'bitter' to describe it. (And it's the same word that often springs to people's lips when tasting tea or coffee, interestingly.) It is their way of qualifying a new taste that is a bit more intense than they are used to. Nine times out of ten, it is not the most accurate word to use. Poor-quality chocolate may be astringent (drying or puckering – like chewing a grape skin).

acidic

Alternatively, what you're tasting (if it doesn't seem sour) may be acidity. Try sniffing something very high in acidity, like vinegar, and notice how the edges of your tongue curl up in anticipation of how it will taste in your mouth. Acidity has a very strong effect on the sides of the tongue. Start smelling things routinely and you will realise how important a component acidity is in everything from milk to fruit.

True *bitterness* is felt in the middle at the back of the tongue. Test it in foods like chicory or grapefruit, to see how your mouth responds. Guanaja from Valrhona is rather bitter, but in such a mild and elegant way you'll hardly feel it.

With some training, you'll even detect chocolates that begin with one flavour (sweetness, for example) and evolve to another (say, bitterness) with a hint of a third (salty) e.g. Lindt 99%.

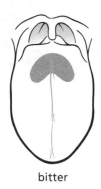

bitter

Saltiness

Saltiness is one of the first tastes you notice, and it lasts longer than sweetness. To familiarise yourself with the effect it has on your tongue, swill some salty water around in your mouth.

Salt is unusual in chocolate but you can find it in some filled chocolates (it enhances the nuttiness in pralines) or in bars like Domori's Latte Sal or 99% Lindt. Here it would be used to reveal particular aromas from the beans or the nuts – in the same way that a little salt brings out the flavour in food.

salty

Describing aromas and flavours

The last part of tasting consists in trying to find the words to describe the aromas and flavours you detect. This is very hard as we are not used to associating a word with a taste sensation. Bite any square of fine dark chocolate, and try to describe the aromas and flavours, not just whether you like it or not. You might not be able to find the words to describe it.

I understand this completely. I've felt it myself, and I've seen it many times in my tasting workshops: you end up with a blank notepad. To make it easier, I suggest you proceed as for a wine tasting: try to find associations with the world around you. When you taste, close your eyes and think, 'What does this remind me of?'

In the beginning, try at least to work out which 'family' the chocolate reminds you of. Use the entries on the inner ring of the chart below as guidance or inspiration.

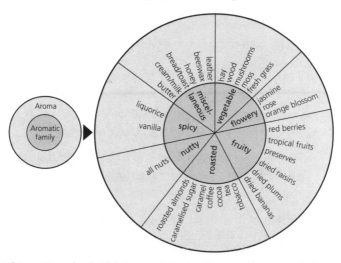

This tasting wheel will help you develop your own choco-vocabulary

Try it yourself! Take a square of Valrhona's Manjari. Pop a small piece into your mouth, and once the initial burst of acidity lowers, see if you can notice the clear red fruit notes.

In the beginning, if you can at least identify 'fruity', this is excellent. Later on, as your ability to identify flavours and aromas grows, you'll be able to fit more specific words to tastes. You can move from tasting Java from Pralus as 'vegetable' to something more accurate, for example, wood or even better, a wet forest.

Find words that sum up what *you* taste, not what you think you should taste, or what someone else has tasted. On a graph, you could draw up one curve for the 'intensity' of the flavours: in their initial attack, in their development, and in their finish. You may taste 'flowery' followed by 'woody' and then 'woody flirting with spicy'.

CHECKLIST FOR TASTING

Try doing the following exercise with a square of chocolate:

1. Look at it: what do you see? Colour? Shine? Texture? Blooming or discolouration?

2. Touch it: what do you feel? How does the broken surface look: smooth or rough and bubbly? Sticky?

3. Listen to it: what do you hear as you snap a square in half?

4. Smell it: what do you find?

5. Taste it: analyse only the texture. Notice its effect on your tongue. How does it feel in your mouth?

The simple approach is a good one to start with, and is what I use in my tasting workshops. If you want to take it further, here is the most traditional tasting method:

1. Put a tiny piece in your mouth, chew it, then stop and allow it to melt.

2. Concentrate on what you feel, and if there is any change in flavour or what your tongue feels over time.

3. Look for flavours:
   a. Do you recognise them?
   b. Do they evolve over time?
   c. Do they interact with each other, or do they seem to come in separate phases? Is one more present and clear than the others, or do they combine?
   d. Rate their intensity.

4. Do you feel any bitterness, acidity or astringency? Do you find it mild or annoying?

5. A good chocolate has three distinct phases. Try to distinguish them:
   a. What you feel in the first seconds
   b. What you feel while it slowly melts
   c. Now swallow: what do you feel now? This phase is called the 'end of mouth'.

6. Rate it: How would you score it globally out of ten?

Remember: all the tastes that you can identify are valid. There's no right or wrong – and nobody is trying to test you or catch you out. No other person has your palate and therefore nobody but you can know what you taste in a chocolate!

Creating the right conditions

I started my analytical tasting regime at the age of 13, when, in Paris, I discovered chocolate was a treasure that deserved the respect and attention of an empty stomach and a clean palate. The longer I left it after eating, the more I could taste in my chocolate, so doing my ritual tasting before breakfast made total sense to me – and I still do my tasting for work at 6 am.

However, I am not suggesting that you have to eat chocolate so early in the day to appreciate it. Everyone has his or her own 6 am – a time in their day when they are at their most sensually alert, and have also gone several hours (I recommend a minimum of two, more after a meal) without eating, or drinking alcohol, juice, fizzy drinks, tea or coffee. You will know, when you read this, what time of day would best suit you and your body: early morning, mid-morning (before a late breakfast), early evening (after a light and early lunch), or late at night (if you tend to eat a light early evening meal).

As I've indicated above, a successful tasting needs 'exam conditions': no smoking, no drinking (except water), silence, paper, pen, an organised table, and a clear action plan in your head. This sounds a bit intimidating, but it will simply facilitate the intimate conversation between you and the chocolate. And nobody is going to mark your paper or judge you!

Before you start, make sure there is no smell or noise to distract you; and be sure that you will not be interrupted for at least half an hour. Your tasting room should be at room temperature (68–74°F), and your body and mind should be calm and comfortable. Ideally, you shouldn't be wearing any perfume or other scent, as this can influence what you taste. A good way to start is to do a bit of yogic breathing, inhaling slowly through your nose and exhaling for the same slow count. Focus on the point between your eyes, empty your mind and relax your neck and shoulders.

ARE YOU READY TO TASTE?

- Is it the right time of day? Do you feel you have left a reasonable period of time since your last snack, meal or hot drink?
- Is it the right place? Are you comfortable and unlikely to be disturbed?
- Is the room at a comfortable temperature?
- Do you have peace and quiet?
- Are you free from interfering smells?
- Are you in the right state of mind – calm, but alert?
- Are you alone or with friends who will work to the same tasting criteria?

Changing tastes...

I meet a lot of would-be chocolate connoisseurs, and I pride myself on my ability to 'bring the choco-light' to anyone willing to discover and enjoy the finest chocolate – whatever their current level of consumption. However, your journey may not be straightforward. Rarely does anyone make a swift move from cheap, sugary milk 'chocolate' to fine dark chocolate. Moreover, I don't recommend that you taste the most unusual chocolates first – it should be a progressive discovery. Your tastes and feelings need to adapt gradually! So, be prepared to give this your time and dedication.

If you have children, remember how long it took them to adjust to each new flavour you tried to introduce when they were babies. You had to keep on giving them tiny tastes before their palate would even begin to accept some foods (some say it takes an average of 12 attempts at tasting something new for a child to begin to find it acceptable, so we should never give up!). Your palate is about to undergo the same shock therapy. What makes you pull a face today may one day become one of the most important bars in your chocolate survival kit (see pages 39–40).

Despite my years of experience, I am not completely beyond this stage myself. There is one company whose philosophy and practices I greatly admire, but who make chocolate that I have never yet been able to enjoy, because its flavour is so new and challenging to me. But I won't reject it. Instead, I take a little bite each day, waiting for the time when the flavours start to speak to me.

Would I give every chocolate sample the same chance? Well, that depends on the sample. In my job I receive a lot of products containing ingredients that do not in my opinion qualify them to use the name chocolate. I also receive chocolates that I know, from first sniff, will never tell me anything about themselves other than that they are mediocre – and often, much worse. What many people call chocolate and what I call chocolate are not even close. When I eat a white chocolate truffle, any ganache made with liqueur, or any low-cocoa content (therefore fatty and sugary) 'chocolate' (and I have to eat a lot of these in my job), I am not even reminded of chocolate!

But have no fear. The chocolate bars I will recommend for your tastings are worth the trouble I am asking you to go to.

Choosing what to taste

Now that you know the methodology, you are ready to start to explore the world of chocolate. But if you walk into a shop, you'll be faced with a massive choice. How should you proceed? Where do you even start?

Look back at the chart in Chapter 2 (page 33). You might not have scaled the heady heights of what I would consider 'quality' chocolate yet, but I can give you a short-cut to the top by telling you what I recommend.

Start with your chocolate profile

When planning your first chocolate tasting session, be completely honest, and pick out the profile from those outlined below that most accurately describes you.

1. You love creamy milk chocolate – Cadbury, Lindt, Toblerone, Galaxy and so on.

TASTING SUGGESTIONS: Compare your very favourite milk chocolate bar with Jivara (Valrhona), Milk (Amedei) and Lait Entier (Weiss).

LOOK FOR: Intensity of sweetness, and taste evolution over time. Did you sense any flavours? For example, can you pick out notes of caramel, milk powder, nuts or vanilla?

TAKING IT FURTHER: Discover the latest trends: Latte Sal (Domori), Hacienda Mangaro Lait (Michel Cluizel), Lindt Milk with cocoa nibs.

2. You have developed a taste for 'the good stuff', but generally buy the same bar.

TASTING SUGGESTIONS: Compare 70% Green & Black (or any fair trade or organic bar of similar percentage cocoa solids) with 70% Lindt, Porcelana (Amedei), Guanaja (Valrhona), and any supermarket-label dark bar.

LOOK FOR: Which ones smell of vanilla flavouring and/or sugar? Can you detect an aromatic palette, or is it mainly sugar that is standing out? Which have a feeling of elegance and harmony in the mouth? Which ones are acidic or bitter?

TAKING IT FURTHER: Carupano and Madagascar (Domori), Claudio Corallo with nibs, Java (Pierre Marcolini).

3. You only like dark chocolate and sample a wide range of bars, but never milk.

TASTING SUGGESTIONS: In this tasting, you'll be sampling the worst end of the dark chocolate market with some of the most divine milk chocolate. Try a supermarket brand dark chocolate bar with Jivara (Valrhona) or Latte Sal (Domori).

LOOK FOR: Pleasure.

TAKE IT FURTHER: Taste more slowly and compare the quality of the milk powders.

You'll notice that the suggestions listed here all include some supermarket brands, and some of the artisan brands. Learning what you like is hard if you only taste things in isolation, and it is very important to compare a few bars at one time – varying qualities, but always tasting similar sorts of chocolate. This enables you to ask more questions of the chocolate and more easily come to your own, informed opinion about it.

---

4. You prefer filled chocolates, and when someone mentions the word 'chocolate' you immediately think of a truffle.

TASTING SUGGESTIONS: You have a sweet tooth – but there's no shame in that. Try the *crème de la crème* of truffles, made with top-quality chocolate and no added flavours. Find a good chocolate shop and ask for advice. Alternatively, if you don't have access to those, go online and order the chocolates I suggest on pages 149–50 for the four-chocolate test. You should make sure you try their best plain milk ganaches (chocolates filled with chocolate – does that make you swoon?!). Also try some fine milk chocolate bars: Jivara (Valrhona), Milk (Amedei) and Lait Entier (Weiss).

LOOK FOR: Does your pleasure mainly come from the sugar, or the flavours?

TAKING IT FURTHER: As for number 1, above.

5. You don't actually like chocolate – at least, you have never found a bar you can enjoy.

I assume that if you are reading this book you are not a chocophobe, but believe me, I have met them! If the reason is that you have more of a savoury than a sweet tooth, let me take you straight to my favourite plantation bars.

TASTING SUGGESTIONS: Manjari (Valrhona), Chuao (Amedei), Claudio Corallo dark chocolate with roasted nibs, Java (Pralus), Porcelana (Domori).

LOOK FOR: Flavours, as you would do for wine. Concentrate on the complexity and evolution of mouth-feel and flavour over time. *Don't* look for pleasure in your first tasting (but maybe in your second one!).

TAKING IT FURTHER: Taste together all Porcelana bars or all Venezuela bars from different brands.

FINESSE YOUR TASTING

- Try to compare a maximum of four chocolates in one sitting (each chocolate will influence the next, so by the time you get to your fourth, your taste buds will be approaching chaos). Drink water or eat bread to cleanse your mouth after each different chocolate.

- Try to compare chocolates of the same colour (all dark, for example, or all milk), and, within that colour, similar percentages (65–75%, for example). If not, the sugar content will prevent a fair comparison of flavours. For example, El Rey's 63%, 70% and 73% all have exactly the same blend of beans. The only difference is the level of sugar, and you will feel as if you are eating three totally different chocolates.

- Always include at least one supermarket bar you are familiar with as a reference. You already know your feelings about this, so it's a way of keeping your feet firmly on the ground when tasting lots of new bars.

- Look back systematically at the checklist for tasting on pages 88–9. Try comparing all the chocolates you are tasting according to these questions. As you become accustomed to different chocolates, levels of acidity and so on, this will start to come more easily to you.

Your tasting may remind you of wonderful or comforting memories from the past – or it may, as it does for me, create a whole story in your head (and the more relaxed and in tune with your mind and body you are, the more this will happen). When you become accustomed to tasting chocolate and articulating your findings, your database of choco sensations will become stored on your brain's hard drive. Not only will you find it easy to fill in your tasting sheet, but images will fill your mind. Your senses will take you to another dimension – even a kind of poetic ecstasy. When I taste Valrhona's Gran Couva Vintage 2003 I feel like I'm dancing among the stars and the angels are smiling at me!

This is a very personal, subjective state, and it's unlikely that two people will 'see' the same things. But, once you have created a chocolate image, it will return whenever you taste that particular chocolate.

SPEED TASTING: FIVE FAST WAYS TO DEVELOP YOUR PALATE

1. Start off slowly... chocolate theme parties are a good way to begin (see the next chapter). Invite friends who share your passion, and get everyone to bring along a new chocolate discovery, or replicate a chocolate dish. (Although, ultimately, only pure unadulterated chocolate will do for formal tastings, at a chocolate party it can be fun and interesting to see how differently people interpret a chocolate tart or cake recipe!) You'll soon find out who among your friends is keen to explore the world of chocolate with you!

2. Make chocolate time special. Get into the habit of eating chocolate away from other food and drink. You know how strange a cup of tea tastes if you have just brushed your teeth with mint toothpaste, or how wine affects the food you eat, and vice versa. Tastes hang around in the mouth for longer than you may realise, and, to fully appreciate chocolate, I recommend leaving at least two hours after a meal. (That's not to say you can't enjoy snacking on chocolate at other times – but, for the purposes of learning to 'taste', make this small sacrifice.)

3. Maximise the pleasure, don't develop cravings. If you tend to crave chocolate for the energy rush it gives you, ask yourself whether something else could satisfy that longing. Is it in fact the sugar rush you want, rather than the chocolate? One way to avoid cravings is to make sure you have a healthy balanced diet. Eating wholefoods (fresh vegetables, pulses, and wholegrains) should keep your blood sugar levels stable and prevent sugar cravings. If you can do this, it will be easier for you to eat chocolate for the pleasure of its chocolate content rather than the sugar it contains (and this is essential when you move on to fine chocolate).

4. Be prepared to pay the price. Good chocolate is expensive. But so is bad chocolate in pretty boxes. Don't get the two mixed up! A simply wrapped bar with a high price tag *and* a reliable name (see column 2 on page 33) will introduce you to the kind of chocolatey tastes that reverberate around the mouth long, long after you've consumed a tiny square.

5. Trust your intuition. Believe in your own opinions, and start forming them. Taste food like a critic. Think about the food you eat and its textures and flavours, and create your own tasting vocabulary. Good wine shops give customers labels with descriptions to alert them to the flavours to expect from selected bottles. Tasting notes are starting to

accompany chocolate sales too. But don't take that taster's word for it. Ask yourself what you think the bar tastes like. What does it remind you of? Does it conjure up an image? If it does, this image will return to you next time you taste the same bar!

Now you know how to taste chocolate, and have a few ideas for tasting combinations, why not make it a social occasion? In the next chapter you'll be able to put your new knowledge to work.

CHAPTER 5

Chocolate to share

*B*UYING NEW CHOCOLATE is tough enough – there's so much to choose from, after all. We've already gone into the countries and regions of origin, and the brands to look for, and I know how daunting all this can be for the novice. So, as I indicated at the end of the last chapter, a fun way to develop your interest in chocolate is to start with themed parties. At these parties, you can invite other chocolate-loving friends, play simple chocolate tasting games with the skills you learned in the last chapter, and serve delicious chocolate dishes. Remember, one of the best ways to really learn and get excited about something new is to share your discoveries and passion with like-minded or interested people.

Chocolate tasting games

You do not have to aspire to becoming a chocolate connoisseur to enjoy the following party games – but you do have to like chocolate!

Here are the ground rules:

- Use all dark, or all milk chocolates, with similar percentages of cocoa solids (try not to have more than 15% difference. For example, if your darkest chocolate is 78% cocoa solids, do not use another in the same game with less than 64% cocoa).

- When setting up the chocolates, try to hide their identities by removing packaging and turning over any surface with a tell-tale sign on it.

- If you are preparing this game, do not take part in it. It is important that no participant has eaten in the last two hours, or drunk tea, coffee or alcohol in the last hour.

Game 1: The Mystery Game

For some suggestions for which chocolates to use for these games, see 'Choosing what to taste' on pages 93–6.

This is very easy to organise and even young children can take part.

Give each participant their own plate with four squares of chocolate. Three are in their original wrapping, or three different colours of paper; one is a mystery square in neutral packaging.

- Cut each square into two pieces. The participants should be instructed to eat half of each of the non-mystery chocolates and then half of the fourth. (*The fourth chocolate is identical to one of three others, but which one? Can your friends work it out?*)

- Now participants should cut each left-over half into two pieces so that they have two-quarters of each on the plate.

- If they have not found out or are not sure which of the two chocolates are identical, start the tasting again, respecting the same order, but this time using only a quarter.

- If they still don't know, you should now reveal the answer and ask the participants to confirm it by tasting the last quarters.

- If they find the answer after the first half, they should use the first quarters to confirm their intuition and keep the last quarters to check the revelation. If they are right, they should just enjoy the last quarter without analysing anything. The aim is to let yourself go with the pleasure and enjoy the boost to your self-esteem!

GAME 2: THE MEMORY GAME

Take four chocolate bars and give each participant a sheet of paper divided into four columns. Allocate three squares of each chocolate bar per column. Using the tasting methodology (see 'The five-sense test' on pages 80–4), fill the columns with your personal tasting notes for each chocolate. The chocolates are then identified and you know which you liked the best and which you would want to add to your desert island suitcase (see pages 38–40). Share your findings.

Two months later … Take two of the same bars of chocolate as before and two new bars. In four columns on a sheet of paper make your tasting notes as before. Can you recognise the chocolates you tasted last time? And how do your new tasting notes compare with your old ones? Have you changed your mind about which chocolate you like best?

One of the ideas about tasting so intently is that you'll develop some clear ideas about your feelings for each chocolate. Gradually, you will build up a stock of information that you'll be able to refer back to. The next time you feel in a particular mood, and 'chocolate' springs to mind, your evolved choco-vocabulary and knowledge of the flavours and sensations each chocolate gave you may help you to pinpoint the exact chocolate you feel like.

At your chocolate theme party, and after your tasting games, why not serve hot chocolate and finish off with a truly sumptuous chocoholic dessert?

Tastes of heaven

What most people expect when they order a cup of hot chocolate is a sweet and milky chocolate drink, with whipped cream on the top. Here are two deliciously different recipes you can whisk up at home.

Ingrid's Spicy Hot Chocolate

MAKES FOUR SERVINGS

For the genuine experience, use exactly the kinds of chocolate and cocoa powder listed here. If you can't find them, do try and replace them with quality alternatives (rather than supermarket brands). It just won't taste the same otherwise! Valrhona cocoa powder can be used in place of Scharffen Berger, for instance.

2¼ cups whole milk
2 to 4 tablespoons mineral or filtered water
½ vanilla bean, split open
pinch ground ginger
pinch ground cinnamon
pinch finely ground black pepper
pinch ground anise
3½ ounces Pralus Trinidad chocolate, finely chopped
3 tablespoons sugar-free Scharffen Berger powdered chocolate
4 to 8 tablespoons sugar
3 tablespoons light cream

1. Heat the milk, water, vanilla bean, ginger, cinnamon, pepper and anise in a saucepan over low heat until hot.

2. Add the chocolate and cocoa, whisking vigorously to prevent the chocolate from sticking to the pan and developing a burnt flavour.

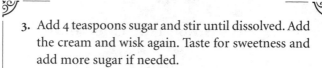

3. Add 4 teaspoons sugar and stir until dissolved. Add the cream and wisk again. Taste for sweetness and add more sugar if needed.

4. Remove from the heat and leave the chocolate to rest in a cool place for up to 45 minutes. Remove the vanilla bean.

5. Return the chocolate to low heat, whisking in air to make it frothy, and heat until hot. Serve immediately.

Hot Chocolate *à la* Chloé

MAKES 4 SERVINGS

If you are more of a traditionalist, and want to taste the ultimate hot chocolate, here is the way I make it.

3½ ounces Michael Cluizel Hacienda chocolate (see notes below)
2¼ cups whole milk
3 tablespoons light cream
6 to 8 teaspoons confectioners' sugar
3 tablespoons Valrhona cocoa powder

1. Coarsely chop the chocolate and set aside.

2. Heat the milk, cream and 6 teaspoons sugar in a saucepan over low heat until hot. Add the chocolate and cocoa to the milk mixture, and whisk until the chocolate pieces have dissolved. Taste for sweetness and stir in more sugar if needed.

3. Cool the mixture slightly, cover and refrigerate for five to six hours for the flavours to blend.

4. Reheat over low heat when you are ready to serve.

Notes:
If you can't find Michel Cluizel chocolate, use Valrhona Guanaja or Noir Gastronomie.

  If you cannot wait six hours, try to give the drink

at least one hour for the flavours to develop. However, six hours will give a much better intensity of flavour.

If you want an easy shortcut, use whole milk, cocoa powder (the best you can find – I recommend Scharffen Berger) and sugar to taste. The flavour will be at its best if you simmer over a low heat for one minute, whisking constantly.

Another truly delicious treat for your party is a chocolate tart. One of the most chocoholic desserts I know, this is almost like a big filled chocolate. But what makes it special is that, unlike a filled chocolate, you can share it.

A changing palate doesn't mean you have to give up on an old friend entirely. Before I became buyer at Fortnum & Mason, I used to eat a spoonful of Nutella each morning before I went for a swim – even long after I decided it wasn't equal in quality to other chocolate I loved.

I no longer eat Nutella, but it retains a special place in my heart. When I moved to London three years ago to start my job, my sister gave me the complete range of 14 oz Nutella jars, each one from a different country. I haven't eaten their contents, but I must admit to taking the occasional sniff, for old times' sake.

DID YOU KNOW?

Nutella was created by Pietro Ferrero (a pastry maker and founder of the Ferrero company) in the 1940s.

- The spread started life as Supercrema Gianduja, and quickly became so popular that, in 1946, Italian stores offered a service called 'smearing' – which allowed local children to bring in a slice of bread on which they could have some Nutella spread.

- The spread changed its name to Nutella in 1964.

- Italy now makes 179,000 tons of it each year. That's 400 million 1lb jars!

- Its recipe, as secret as Coca-Cola's, has never been matched by any other chocolate spread.

- Even if the list of ingredients is long and a bit mundane-sounding – sugar, vegetable oil, hazelnuts, fat-reduced cocoa powder, skimmed milk powder, whey powder, soy lecithin and flavouring – its taste and smell are seductive.

- Nutella outsells all the world's brands of peanut butter put together – if you look in the luggage of any travelling Italian businessman, you're likely to find a jar of Nutella in there, a welcome reminder of home!

Nutella Tart

MAKES 12 SERVINGS

I came across my first Nutella Tart at my sister's 21st birthday party. It was delicious, and I quickly worked out a shortcut version. Simply buy a 9- or 10-inch graham-cracker pie shell and fill it with the contents of a 470g (about 17-ounce) jar of Nutella (double if you plan to lick the spatula!). A more sophisticated version of the Nutella Tart appears in Délices d'Initiés, *a book of recipes using children's ingredients, written by Frédérick E. Grasser-Hermé, wife of Parisian chocolatier Pierre Hermé. The recipe was created with me and my passion for Nutella in mind!*

FOR THE PASTRY
10 tablespoons (5 ounces) butter, softened
4 tablespoons ground almonds
¾ cup confectioners' sugar
pinch sea salt
1 teaspoon vanilla extract
3 large eggs
2 cups all-purpose flour

FOR THE FILLING
½ cup Nutella hazelnut spread
5 ounces dark chocolate (such as Valrhona Caraïbe), melted
1 large egg
2 large egg yolks
2 tablespoons superfine sugar
8 tablespoons (4 ounces) unsalted butter, melted and warm

1. To make the pastry: Whisk the butter so it's evenly blended. Add the almonds, sugar, salt and vanilla. Beat in the eggs. Stir in the flour, mixing just until the dough comes together. Wrap the dough in plastic wrap and refrigerate it for one hour.

2. Preheat the oven to 350°F. Gently press the dough into a 10- or 11-inch tart pan with a removable bottom. (This is a thick crust.) Line with aluminum foil and add pie weights or dried beans. Bake for about 25 minutes, or until edges are brown and center springs back when pressed. Remove foil and pie weights.

3. To make the filling: Combine the ingredients in the order in which they appear in the list. Pour the filling into the tart shell. Bake for about 15 minutes, or until the center of the filling is still soft but the edge of the filling is set. Cool until warm and serve.

Note:
This tart is best eaten on the day of cooking, but leftovers can be refrigerated for two to three days. It should be brought to room temperature before serving.

Ingrid's Tarte au Chocolat

*This wonderful chocolate tart recipe is from my friend,
Ingrid Astier.*

FOR THE PASTRY
6 tablespoons (3 ounces) butter, softened
5 tablespoons sugar
1 large egg
1¼ cups all-purpose flour
2 tablespoons cornmeal
2 tablespoons ground almonds
pinch sea salt
pinch ground cinnamon
seeds from ½ vanilla bean or 1 teaspoon vanilla extract

FOR THE FILLING
1⅔ cups heavy cream
pinch ground cinnamon
pinch ground ginger
1 Tahitan vanilla bean, split open
¾ cup confectioners' sugar
14 ounces dark chocolate (Ingrid uses half Pralus Ghana
and half Pralus Java, but use the best you can find)
1 ounce Jivara chocolate (a Valrhona milk chocolate)
1 tablespoon butter, in small pieces
2 tablespoons toasted, crushed hazelnuts

1. To make the pastry: Mix the butter (which should be quite soft) with the sugar. When this is well blended, beat in the egg. Add the flour, cornmeal, almonds, salt, cinnamon and vanilla seeds to the mixture. Work the dough into a ball, cover with plastic wrap, and refrigerate it for two hours.

2. Preheat the oven to 350°F. Gently press the dough into a 10-inch tart pan with a removable bottom. Line with foil and add pie weights or dried beans. Bake for 15 minutes. Remove foil and pie weights and bake about 10 minutes, or until lightly browned. Let cool.

3. To make the filling: Bring the cream to a boil with the cinnamon, ginger and vanilla bean. Turn off the heat as soon as the mixture boils. Let stand for 15 minutes to infuse and then remove the vanilla bean. Bring to a boil again and turn off the heat.

4. Make a caramel by warming the confectioners' sugar in a saucepan until golden (but being careful not to burn it). Return the cream to low heat and add the caramel, stirring to dissolve. Once the caramel is dissolved in the cream, take the pan off the heat.

5. Chop all the chocolate into pieces and place it in a heat-proof bowl. Slowly pour the hot caramel-cream mixture over the chocolate, whisking it in but without adding too much air. When the mixture is lukewarm, add the butter in batches, and mix carefully.

6. Place the hazelnuts in the tart shell. Slowly pour the filling over the hazelnuts. Cool for three hours, or until set, before eating.

Note: This tart is best eaten on the day of cooking, but leftovers can be refrigerated for two to three days. It should be brought to room temperature before serving.

An eighteenth-century French print of vanilla pods

Now that you know how good chocolate is made, and how it tastes, you are probably beginning to understand why I am so keen to introduce fine chocolate to as many people as possible, and why each little introduction means so much to me.

·

CHAPTER 6

The cream of the crop

IF YOU ARE READY to follow me in the discovery of 'real' chocolate – the cream of the crop – my advice is simple. Try new chocolates as often and as conscientiously as you can, tasting them (and not just 'eating' them), and following the methodology in the last chapter.

I truly believe that each one of us has gourmet potential, and that all you need is the opportunity to wake it up and educate it.

But first you need to understand what you are up against, and why, to a certain extent, you will have to turn detective to find the kind of quality chocolate I am urging you to taste.

To recap: the truth about chocolate

Here are the facts:

The world produces around 3 million tons of cocoa beans per year and Africa (Ivory Coast and Ghana mainly) provides seventy per cent of that total, using beans from

Forastero trees, which as you'll remember is the least aromatic of the cocoa family.

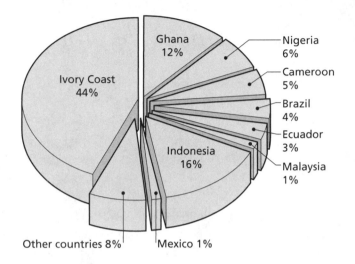

World cocoa-bean market

The aromatic quality of the resulting chocolate depends on:

1. The bean that it is made from – they must be beans with a good aromatic potential

2. How these beans are fermented

3. How the beans are dried

4. How these beans are conched

An estimated 15 % of world production:
Good Beans (e.g. Criollo/Trinitario hybrid or
Trinitario) + good fermentation = good chocolate
Good Beans + bad fermentation = bad chocolate

An estimated 85 % of world production:
Poor Beans (e.g. Forastero) + good fermentation =
poor chocolate
Poor Beans + bad fermentation = terrible
chocolate!

The incredible truth ... most chocolate isn't great

Ninety per cent of the world's cocoa beans come from farms less than five hectares in size: that is to say, places where farmers ferment their beans in their backyard or take them to the nearest co-operative where, with no attention to ripeness or quality variations, all the local beans are mixed up and fermented together.

This fermentation process is usually too short for the proper development of the precursors of aromas to take place, because the co-operatives need cash fast.

Most of these poor beans are purchased and processed into chocolate by four main multinational groups, who supply the vast majority of the chocolate companies we know. When selecting their beans, they concentrate on size and lack of flaws rather than aromatic properties – the very same process that perpetuates the sale of those big, tasteless, ruby-red tomatoes you can buy in the supermarket.

The aroma-inducing conching process first used by Lindt lasted for three days. Only a few fine chocolate producers still conch for this length of time, as the multinationals push for 'more efficient' and shorter conching times.

You'll probably have a good idea where I am coming from now when I say that in my opinion, 90 per cent of the chocolate available to us ranges from uninteresting to horrendous (bad beans and/or bad processing)! The problem is that the majority of this poor chocolate is dressed up with marketing, labelling and packaging and presented as good chocolate.

I've recommended a number of top-quality chocolates. But what I haven't yet covered are the 'wolves in sheep's clothing' of the chocolate world. These have all the 'right' words on the label and aren't cheap. They are cleverly marketed – but they are an inferior product.

So how do you recognise friend from foe? Well, there is no other way than to taste. And taste again. *Think* as you taste … and learn to trust your taste buds. Only they can tell you if what you are eating is *true* quality or if it is a smartly marketed impostor. On the following pages I'll give you more information that will help you to distinguish between good and bad.

COUVERTURE

Did you know that the vast majority of the brands we see in supermarkets, the Belgian chocolates Godiva and Leonidas, and Thornton's, as well as the small artisan chocolatiers, all buy the same raw material?

Chocolatiers buy chocolate in bulk, called 'couverture', rather than grinding their own cocoa beans. Couverture can take the form of ready-to-melt chocolate in big blocks of 2 to 55 lbs. In addition to this packet form, couverture can also be bought as liquid chocolate, which has been pre-melted and tempered. The liquid form is even easier for chocolatiers to work with as it is ready to be moulded. It is kept at 113°F and distributed in tank trucks. (Those trucks look so much like the ones used to transport milk or petrol that whenever I see one on the road, I end up imagining it filled with one of my favourite chocolates!)

So when you buy a few bars, say two single-estate bars from Madagascar, made by different brands, nine times out of ten the manufacturers will have had a choice of only two different couvertures. The two bars you've bought might actually have come from the same bulk chocolate! Chocolate makers do this because it's not cost-efficient to grind beans themselves. More than half the world's bean production is transformed into chocolate by just four multinationals: ADM, Cargill, Barry Callebaut and Nestlé. We all know Nestlé, but only professionals know the others – as these multinationals only sell to professionals. The bad news is that the groups who buy the beans have no real interest in aromas: when selecting the beans, they concentrate only on size and lack of flaws.

All the big companies that you've heard of offer a wide range of quality. But I find even their top of the range 'single-estate beans' couvertures far less exciting than premium-quality ones from Valrhona, Pralus, Cluizel, Amedei and Domori. The problem is that chocolatiers would need to pay from two to four times as much for these. And although they want to keep their customers happy, they also like to make money from their business.

If customers enjoy and keep on buying chocolate that I would consider to be of inferior quality, then there is little incentive for the melters of couverture to invest in a more expensive chocolate.

A 1929 advertisement from Nestlé for milk chocolate

CHOC-FULL OF GOODNESS!

Reading the ingredients list

As you know by now, the basic raw materials to make a dark chocolate bar are beans (*cocoa* on the ingredients list) and sugar. These were the ingredients used in the very first bar created by Fry's in 1847. Cocoa butter began to be added later that century, and lecithin after World War II. You also know that since Mayan times, vanilla was often added to the beans mixture. Today, most of the bars sold on the mass market have a much longer ingredients list – and reading labels of the bars in your local supermarket is an astonishing experience I recommend to any choco-explorer.

But what does cocoa percentage really mean? A 70% cocoa solids bar means that 70 per cent of the total weight comes from cocoa beans. For example, if you take a Pralus 70% bar, you will read 'cocoa, sugar, cocoa butter, lecithin and vanilla'. The 100g bar has been made by combining 2 oz beans, 1/4 oz cocoa butter and 1 oz sugar (the weight of the lecithin and vanilla are negligible).

In your mission to spy on as many labels as you can, do not forget that ingredients lists appear in decreasing quantities. You are not at the end of your surprises. The ingredients list of a very famous American milk chocolate bar starts with … 'milk chocolate' ! Once you recover from the shock of discovering that milk chocolate is made with milk chocolate, I suggest you continue reading. Between a set of brackets you can then read: sugar, milk, cocoa butter, chocolate (finally we found you, dear beans!), lecithin and vanillin. *You* are expert enough now to know that 'chocolate' means 'cocoa'. But the fact that there is more sugar than cocoa is the final knife in the connoisseur's heart. In the US, you can legally describe as milk chocolate a product that has at least 10% cocoa content (that is, cocoa butter *and* beans). Our culprit here probably only contains 4% cocoa beans!

READ THAT WRAPPER

Take a look at the back of a bar you have at home. You will probably find most of the following words:

- Cocoa: ground cocoa beans.

- Sugar.

- Cocoa butter: We know by now that a chocolate bar is made from ground beans and added cocoa butter. Usually the amount of cocoa butter is the equivalent of around 10 per cent of the weight of the ground beans.

- Lecithin: an emulsifier, added to ensure the ingredients are blended evenly.

- Vanilla/vanillin: Vanilla is the real thing. Any company using vanilla will probably announce it proudly as 'natural vanilla pods' or similar. Vanillin, on the other hand, is a cheap synthetic version of vanilla that pollutes the aromas the beans could have brought, or is added to hide the unpleasant bad aromas of cheap beans. In all cases, it means the brand decided to cut costs, and ultimately quality.

It is when you start reading ingredients such as lactose, whey powder, cocoa powder, malt extract, butter fat, emulsifiers (other than soy lecithin) that your alarm-bells should start ringing. Cocoa powder in a dark chocolate is very suspicious. Sadly, this does not prevent brands which include cocoa powder from pricing their product at a premium and calling it 'Finest dark chocolate' – and charging accordingly.

DID YOU KNOW?

There is a legal definition of chocolate related to the percentage of dry cocoa solids and the percentage of cocoa butter. They are not the same for every country. There are several different grades of chocolate, and these figures show the European Union and US regulations for standard (S) as well as fine (F) chocolate.

- Dark chocolate (S) must contain at least 35% dry cocoa solids (but 15% for 'sweet chocolate' in the US), while dark chocolate (F) must contain at least 43%.

- Milk chocolate (S) must contain at least 25% dry cocoa solids (but 20% in the UK, and 10% in the US), while fine milk chocolate must contain at least 30%.

Bars such as Cadbury Dairy Milk, Galaxy or Hershey must be labelled 'family milk chocolate' in the EU, as they don't contain enough chocolate to count as chocolate under these rules!

But what about the cocoa butter content? This substance is a commodity in its own right, used in cosmetics as well as chocolate. And it's expensive, at least ten times more than the vegetable fats used to replace it, known as cocoa butter equivalents (or CBEs).

Since a European ruling that up to 5 per cent of the total weight of a chocolate bar can be made of non-cocoa fats, many mass-market manufacturers are using CBEs. Do you want to know what they are? Take a deep breath ... palm oil, illipe (bomeo tallow or tengkawang), sal, shea, kokum gurgi and mango kernel. They don't sound very appetising to me!

Organic – is it worth it?

There is one final thing to be said about what to look for in chocolate. We live in an age when the word 'organic' makes people go weak at the knees. If a chocolate is organic, it is perceived as being healthier, less of a sin, and, therefore, more acceptable than the non-organic specimen next to it. Then there's the fact that organic and fair trade usually go hand in hand – so your money is helping to maintain a healthy environment *and* ensuring that co-operatives receive a good price for their product . . . and many of us like to buy organic for just this reason.

The truth is that when you buy organic, you are buying a product certified to have been grown or made according to specific criteria: the beans, cocoa butter, and the sweetener (organic cane sugar or evaporated cane juice) have been grown without pesticides, are not genetically modified and are free from artificial additives. But I do wonder how organic bean brokers can afford *not* to spray their beans with pesticides when transporting them (and in all likelihood lose part of their shipment) when they sell them as cheaply as anyone else.

Whatever the criteria the ingredients conform to, the chain of production is no different to that of any old common or garden chocolate. It is not, as consumers believe, 'made by manufacturers who pick their own beans from co-operatives in producing countries'.

For a start, most organic brands do not begin with their own beans. They buy various couvertures (bulk chocolate) from big companies, selecting the ones they want to blend for each specific bar, melting, mixing, tempering and moulding them. They belong in the melters category.

The ingredients of the couverture they buy are, of course, organic, and the beans come from certified fair-trade co-operatives – but there are very few of these and producing a quality aromatic bean is not their priority. In fact, only two or three countries have had any of their bean production certified as organic – so you can imagine there's not much for the organic brands to choose from.

You may have noticed that within an organic dark range there are rarely more than two different types of plain bars (what I would consider 'real' chocolate). And this is the reason why – they just don't have enough beans to choose from. That's why most organic brands have a wide range of fancy bars, filled with liquid flavourings or mixed with orange, spices or nuts.

I have met a lot of organic 70% eaters on my chocolate courses. Some are 'exclusively organic products people', who usually indulge in the whole range, fancy bars included. But most of them are health-conscious people, who rejected supermarket milk chocolate long ago as too sweet and fatty, and moved to dark chocolate with a high percentage of cocoa solids. For them, when organic chocolate came on the scene it was another great boost for health.

I am always reminded of a 1997 meeting of the French chocolate society, the *Club des Croqueurs du Chocolat*, where we had a blind tasting of six samples of dark chocolate bars, all around 70% cocoa solids. None of us liked any of the chocolates we'd been given, unanimously describing them as 'astringent, acidic, harsh, grainy'. When their identities were revealed, it emerged that they were all organic.

I probably won't make any friends when I say this but every time I eat organic chocolate a little voice in my head says: 'Just let me give a cheque to the co-operative, but please don't make me eat this!' What I look for in chocolate is pleasure, and the day organic chocolate gives me the same thrills as fine chocolate, I will add it to my survival kit.

However, if you do really want to support these companies and like fruit and nut bars, the ones I recommend are the Green & Black range, Dagoba (an American brand), and the quinoa and dark chocolate bar by Kaoka of France. Wherever you live, you can purchase them over the web (see page 211)

The future for organic

So what's the future for organic chocolate? As the demand for it increases, production is increasing too. Many medium-size bean producers all over the world sniffed a good opportunity two or three years ago and signed up for organic certification. Nearly all the producers I came across are about to be certified. This is very good news as it means that organic chocolate manufacturers will have more and more choice in terms of beans – so we can expect higher quality and more flavourful beans in the future.

But what I'm really interested in are the few companies who have bought their own plantations to ensure quality.

Companies such as Dagoba, aware of the quality gap in organic chocolate, are keen to improve the quality of their product right along the line, from fermentation to bar.

Pleasure and *profit*

Now that you have started to taste real chocolate, can you tell the difference between good and bad quality? Would you be prepared to pay more so that chocolatiers could afford to use the better-quality raw material that would push their prices up? They need to know you are on their side before they will take this risk.

But, as the revolution takes off, I am confident that more and more consumers will be aware of the quality it is possible to get, and will be more fussy. Eventually even the most profit-oriented chocolatiers will be pressed to demand finer ingredients from their suppliers – and more and more of us will be willing to pay for the pleasure.

And I hope that you will be there, to check who's producing the best chocolate!

CONNOISSEUR'S CORNER...

I eat more than a pound of chocolate a day, but none of it from the 95 per cent that makes up the majority of the world's chocolate. I only eat the best. When you have tasted quality, whether in food or wine, there's no going back.

Over the years I have created my database of 'chocopleasures', the same way one creates a music library. When I find a CD I like, I buy it and listen to it whenever I feel like it. My relationship with chocolate is similar but, as an expert, I try every new release, and take the time to analyse any that seems worth the trouble. I keep a track of all the chocolate that really deserves the name *chocolate* because of what I know about that company's production techniques, sourcing of beans, the chocolate's aromas, and, to some extent, whether I like them or not (I can't like everything – but I can recognise quality even if I do not like it!). I do this because I need to be able to refer to my database to check things I hear about different bars, or compare one bar with the sensations another one gives me.

Creating your database will open a whole new dimension in your journey in the chocolate world. The more attention you give chocolate when you taste it, the more you will be able to feel at any new tasting, the more you will be able to establish links with past tastings. A few examples of what you will be able to do as a connoisseur are:

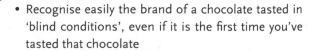

- Recognise easily the brand of a chocolate tasted in 'blind conditions', even if it is the first time you've tasted that chocolate

- Be able to refer to other chocolates to compare them with the ones you are analysing (it has the same level of acidity as X but with a texture closer to Y and lingers much longer in the mouth than X or Y)

- Tell easily between 'good' and 'bad' – your taste buds are far more discerning than your wallet.

CHAPTER 7

.

Bars and bonbons

I OFTEN TALK ABOUT chocolate and chocolates – to distinguish between chocolate bars and filled chocolates. As you know, the connoisseur concentrates on the bar. But perhaps, in *your* heart, you concentrate on the bonbon! There is nothing more thrilling for more than a few of us than a beautiful box of chocolates.

Let's look at the exciting developments bubbling away in the world of bars, and of bonbons.

Bars with a difference

I've been talking about the chocolate revolution. Now let's see how quality chocolate-makers are experimenting with new varieties of chocolate, and new labelling methods – along with some of the huge companies that supply the supermarkets.

In the last two decades we've seen startling changes in chocolate. The timeline opposite gives some idea of these seismic shifts.

As you can see, between the first ever bar and the 1980s, not a great deal happened. Once the technology was in place, nobody rocked the boat – but then when changes finally did begin to creep in (1985), everyone else followed suit. You can see the proliferation of fine-quality bars over the last 20 years. Also interesting to track is how the big brands have followed suit with similar bars, but not until five to ten years later! However, as the chocolate revolution speeds up, the larger brands have become much faster to copy successes.

1815: Van Houten isolates cocoa butter

1847: Fry invents the first solid chocolate bar: beans, sugar and cocoa butter

1879: Conching is invented, improving texture and coaxing more flavour from the beans

1920: The first bar affordable for all is available

1983: Bonnat introduce single-estate bars

1984: Bonnat introduces a 50% milk bar

1986: Valrhona's first bar, Guanaja, is released

1988: Valrhona's Caraïbe bar

1989: Lindt's 70% Noir

chart continues

1992: Lindt's country-of-origin bars

1994: Weiss & Chaudun's dark bar with cocoa nibs
Bonnat's Hacienda el Rosario (the first plantation bar)

1998–9: Michel Cluizel's Nuanciers
Valrhona's Gran Couva (the second plantation bar)

2000: Michel Cluizel's Hacienda Concepcion (plantation bar)

2001: Lindt's Éclats de Fèves
Bonnat's milk, 65%, country-of-origin bar
Lindt's 99% bar

2002: Michel Cluizel's Hacienda Los Ancones (plantation bar)
Valrhona's Amanpakia (plantation bar)

2003: Domori's Puertomar, the first pure Criollo bar

2004: Michel Cluizel's Hacienda Mangaro Lait

Every year, the mass market brands launch bars with new and dramatic flavour combinations – so nearly every filling or combination of tastes you could imagine seem to grace the supermarket shelves. And there's another trend. Instead of just the traditional range of milk, dark and many different varieties of nutty, fruity, fancy, flavoured and filled chocolate bars, you might be seeing new additions on the shelves of your local supermarket or deli. They are plain and look very much, at least in terms of the labelling, like the ones we see at the more expensive end of the market.

What's on the label?

Once, 70% chocolate was the reigning favourite, and for many people it still is. But percentages are no longer the *only* way to distinguish between different varieties of dark and milk chocolate. And, in fact, there are more and more different types of plain chocolate bars creeping onto the shelves, with very different pieces of information on the label: country of origin, plantation, bean variety and vintage (but not, sometimes, the percentage).

You know, now, how much difference there can be between different varieties of cocoa bean. But it doesn't end there. Think of wine again. Many of the grape varieties that are grown to make wine have been planted in different wine-growing regions. For example, you might find the same grape growing in parts of Australia, California and France. The resulting wines, because of varying elements in the grapes' environment (the *terroir*) and treatment, are extremely different. The same goes for chocolate. So the region or plantation where the beans come from is quite important knowledge!

Origins

The different brands label their chocolate in several ways, giving more or less information:

- Plantation bars, such as Valrhona's Gran Couva – denoting beans which come exclusively from just one plantation (a few acres of land).

- Single-estate bars, such as Chuao, which is a region of Venezuela.

- Country-of-origin bars, such as Lindt's Ghana, Madagascar and Ecuador bars. These beans come from anywhere within the named country.

As far as I'm concerned, the more you know, the better. I can tell you from my own tastings that bars made from Venezuelan beans are better than those made from Ecuadorian beans, but the truth is that bad beans can come from Venezuela, and vice versa. (Just as you can buy cheap, horrendous French wine – the country alone is not enough to mean anything, in terms of quality.) If you look for labels with more information, rather than less, you will have a clearer idea of what you're actually buying.

As we saw at the start of this book, there are moves for wine terminology to be used more and more in the chocolate world. Some are for this, others against – but it is certainly true that some *ideas* from the wine world are useful, and being taken up by chocolate makers and plantation owners with gusto – for example, protecting the origin of the wine with legislation (in wine, it's called AOC, *Appellation d'Origine Controlée*), meaning 'guarantee of controlled origin'). The region of Chuao is a label of quality.

THE CHUAO BEANS

Chuao is a coastal region north of Caracas in Venezuela, well known for its quality beans. It is said that in the seventeenth century the Chuao plantation was given by an aristocratic Spanish woman to the Jesuits so they could make money from the cocoa to build schools and churches. Chuao, isolated by the mountains and the sea, has unique beans that have never been cross-pollinated with other varieties, and these are fermented and dried according to specific local criteria. They are very sought-after. Several high-quality brands sell Chuao single-origin bars, but Amedei from Italy signed a contract a few years ago with the Chuao plantation, buying all their beans for the next few years. This means that legally, as with AOC in wine, Amedei are now the only company who can use the name Chuao for a chocolate. The first Amedei Chuao chocolate arrived on our shelves in 2004. Amedei pay above the odds for Chuao beans in order to ensure quality and you can be assured that if you buy an Amedei Chuao bar, it really will contain the wonderful Chuao beans!

In 1998 Valrhona took the associations with wine even further, and launched a bar whose label had the same layout and vocabulary as used on fine wine labels – including information on the plantation, the origin of the bean, the vintage and the type of chocolate. You will only find the percentage on the back – in small letters! Many other companies have followed suit since those days, and today you can often find this bean-related information on a label.

Vintage (or 'grand cru') is another wine concept that has been increasingly applied to specialist chocolates in recent years. Vintage denotes the year of the cocoa crop, and pays homage to the fact that cocoa beans (and therefore the chocolate made from them) can and should taste different from one year to another. Supermarket brands, on the other hand, spend years perfecting their formula – creating a recipe for chocolate that means the same bar will taste exactly the same at all times.

More and more, labels include tasting notes on them – a brief list of the flavours that you might be able to distinguish. Don't take them too seriously, but use them for inspiration!

Champions of the chocolate bar

I have wonderful contacts in the chocolate world, many of whom are hardly known so far – they are working behind the scenes to bring the best out of chocolate, to reinvent chocolate. Here are some of the most important.

Steve de Vries is a former glassblower who became interested in chocolate in 1999 after visiting Costa Rica. He returned home to Denver with 66 lbs of cocoa beans in his luggage! Steve made his first chocolate in his kitchen, using a grain grinder he'd had for 25 years. His first attempt was a crude, gritty product that was nevertheless swimming with flavours he'd never before come across in any industrial chocolate.

Since then he has worked relentlessly to learn more and more about chocolate. He's visited factories and plantations, experimented with new drying methods, and followed botanists round the Mexican jungle (hunting for 'wild Criollo genes'!). He follows the most advanced courses on the technology of chocolate and attends the latest symposiums. He is passionate about improving and optimising the flavour of chocolate, and is currently experimenting with different chocolate fermenting, drying and tempering methods to this end. He is even revising the traditional texture of chocolate.

He says: 'My approach is to try to make the best chocolate *possible* and a large part of that is to discover what is possible, with very little if any consideration for practicality. And that is why I will happily continue to do things like sun-drying cocoa beans in the manner I've seen in Venezuela, and try to make a chocolate with no added cocoa butter, or vanilla, and with a new texture, as in the 1890s.'

Steve works alone and his chocolate will not be on the market until 2005, but his discoveries will, I believe, be influential.

Claudio Corallo created, in partnership with Pralus, Pralus's plantation bar. Like me, Claudio studied tropical agronomy, and at one time owned a plantation producing coffee of an extremely high quality. But the political situation in Zaïre, where he was based, became so bad that he had to leave, losing everything. He went to São Tomé and started all over again with a new coffee plantation – but this one also had cocoa trees. He now has several plantations growing both coffee and cocoa. His approach is a perfectionist one, working with the locals, and running his business as a co-operative.

Claudio also makes his own chocolate, working miracles with beans that are generally regarded as not of the highest quality – São Tomé has only Forastero trees. He is taking a fresh look at the fermentation and drying process, just as Steve is, to see if different or more intense flavours can be created with different methods.

I got to see some of the process at firsthand when I was staying with his family. They left three plates out in the living room, each holding different cocoa nibs, coded and named. They were there to be tasted at random, and each time any one of us tasted a bean, we were to jot down notes on it. We would then gather to discuss our tasting notes and opinion of each. Claudio is putting his cocoa beans through the same painstaking selection process through which he discovered his superb coffee. (And the process? Each day for five days, he drinks coffee made from the beans of just one tree. After five days, he decides whether to keep the tree – or cut it down!)

He now has a range sold exclusively at Fortnum & Mason in London: three plain chocolates, two with nibs, and the fancy range with ginger, orange or coffee. Every week Claudio air-freights me different chocolates – he is constantly experimenting with processes or different ratios of ingredients, and his chocolate is very much a work in progress. But the improvements he is making, and the amazing results he gets, suggest to me that in years to come Claudio will be one of the biggest names in chocolate.

Domori: The Italian company Domori, founded by Gianluca, is reviving the pure Criollo bean in partnership with the owners of a plantation, grafting Criollos from a gene bank in Trinidad onto local Trinitarios. They plotted a planting schedule that will allow them to release a new bar from their plantation every year, made with a different variety of bean every time. Domori chocolates are much more easily available than those of Steve de Vries and Claudio Corallo – you can mail order them from anywhere in the world.

The path these three people have chosen to take perfectly summarises what I believe will be the next trend in the chocolate world, and as a connoisseur, you have to be up to date with the latest!

Revolution…or revival?

Why are these revolutionaries so special, then? Do they also use revolutionary machinery? To produce a chocolate they want to be different to any they've tasted in the past, they question each step in the process from bean to bar, rejecting or revising it as they consider necessary. Bean varieties, fermentation, drying, the ingredients and even the type of machinery used are all up for scrutiny.

Steve, for example, has travelled the world to buy machinery that looks as if it's been stolen from a museum. He is convinced that old machines were designed to get the most of the bean's potential, and that industrialisation, focusing on the speed and volume, doesn't pay enough attention to flavour. Others look at the old machines for inspiration – Domori and Corallo have both invented their own machines.

And the reason for this old-is-new trend? A few visionaries realised there must be more to chocolate than the mass-produced kind, and went about trying to create chocolate that seems truly different to the smooth and creamy, sugary and vanillin-enriched bars that are so prevalent. Using old machinery, a producer is more likely to be able to treat the beans with the respect they deserve, coaxing as much flavour out of them as possible, allowing them some individuality in their texture.

The mélangeur is an old-style grinding machine

Along with this machinery comes the revival of various types of trees. Domori, Corallo, and Steve work on the quality of the bean from the plantations all the while. They are not alone – and growing numbers of chocolate makers are now going back to the source, either encouraging growers to revive old varieties, or also buying their own plantations.

In each case, these chocolate makers care more for flavour than for time or money, aiming to produce the best chocolate in the world. And what I have experienced so far is indeed totally new – the aromas, the flavours, the texture, the pleasure.

The bars of the future, enriched by so much innovation and experimentation every step of the way, are likely to be even more amazing than today's. If you're like me, you might find it hard to wait!

The best bonbons

As a purist – and as you've seen – I tend to encourage people to taste chocolate rather than chocolates. Bars, instead of bonbons, in short. Chocolate contains the full array of flavours and is the equivalent of fine wine, coffee, or tea, while chocolates are a new and different product, of which chocolate is only one ingredient, and not even the major one.

A chocolate connoisseur is unlikely to eat many chocolates. For example, from the one pound of chocolate I eat a day, barely 2 oz is chocolates – the rest is either plain bars or bars with nuts. As far as I'm concerned, a bar of chocolate is the real thing, cocoa in its most concentrated form, and chocolates are just a diluted (or even polluted) form of chocolate.

If that sounds extreme, I hasten to say that a good filled chocolate *can* be a divine experience. You can probably guess my criteria by now. If the chocolatier is a quality freak, fuelled by real passion for their product, then yes, a wonderful filled chocolate is possible. Of course, as with chocolate bars, there are fine-and poor-quality filled chocolates. As a connoisseur, you need to know the tips to recognise glitter from gold.

Bonbon bonanza

There is no legal definition of chocolates as there is for chocolate (see pages 123–4). Almost anything sweet that has a filling and is coated with chocolate ends up being called a chocolate. Chocolates can, however, be separated into four main categories, based on the composition of the filling. Each of these may come coated in either milk, white or dark chocolate.

- *Ganaches:* these have a soft chocolate filling made with pure chocolate and cream (and many other ingredients when flavoured, or there's a need for a long shelf life).

- *Pralinés* (pronounced 'pralin-ey'): the filling of these looks like the texture of peanut butter, and is made from a mixture of caramel ground together with roasted almonds and/or hazelnuts. Cocoa butter, dark chocolate or milk chocolate may also be added to the filling, influencing the texture. If the filling includes only cocoa butter, it will remain the colour of the praliné. Beware of mistaking *pralines* for *pralinés*. The former is a Belgian word used for all filled chocolates. *Praliné* is the French word (adopted by professionals around the world) used to describe a chocolate made with the mixture described above. The word is also used to refer to the raw material of the praliné mixture.

- *Marzipan:* this filling is a mixture of roasted almonds or hazelnuts ground with sugar (not caramel this time – hence its whitish colour).

- *Others:* I call this category the choco-candies, as in most cases there is not a gram of chocolate in the filling.

Belonging to this category are nougat, Turkish delight, caramels, fudges and English creams.

These are the chocolates you'll be able to pick up at the counter of any chocolatier. Later in this chapter I'll give you a guided tour of a typical chocolates counter (see pages 149–50).

CHALLENGING CREAMS

As my chocolate education is mainly French, I find the ever-popular English rose and violet creams to be a major challenge! The first time I cut one in two and tasted the filling alone (a connoisseur tasting method – see pages 150–52), I had the feeling I had swallowed soap (albeit a fine one!). I guess that, as with Marmite, you need to grow up eating them to love them. Every year, Buckingham Palace orders sumptuous fabric boxes of chocolates for foreign presidents on official visits. I wish I could see the face of the French one biting his first cream!

Making chocolates great

Chocolate is a complex, wayward and fascinating ingredient to work with. Many French chocolatiers have fallen in love with chocolate and left the pastry world to devote their career to it. It is a wonderful arena for a creative mind – but it demands far more than just quality ingredients. This pursuit requires extraordinary skill.

So, when looking for fine chocolates, you need to look both at the quality of the ingredients the chocolatier or manufacturer is using, and how well they are used. You might call it looking for a spark of genius.

Cocoa butter, for example, which gives chocolate its high fat content and melting quality, is unstable at best. The chocolatier needs to understand the way it behaves when heated or when mixed with other ingredients.

But there is naturally more to a filled chocolate than just mixing up the ingredients. I call chocolatiers 'alchemists of pleasure'. Like a 'nose' in the perfume world, the chocolatier is always sniffing out different aromas, creating new pieces of art. How well the chocolatier masters the art of mixing chocolate with other ingredients determines to a large extent whether or not he stands out from the crowd.

Combining several perfectly matching or interestingly harmonious scents can create something sublime, even otherworldly, in the right hands. Take French chocolatier Jacques Genin. Jacques is one of the most talented chocolate makers I have ever met. Based in Paris, he sells only to people who 'get' his product – in fact, you have to pass his tasting test before you are allowed to buy from him! He also supplies the best hotels and restaurants in Paris (…but only once they have passed his test!).

Jacques' tiny workshop is almost impossible to find: there is no door handle, no sign, not even a number. And yet he is known as one of the world's best chocolatiers. He is a perfectionist, and loves chocolate deeply – not only its taste but also its feeling, its shine and its texture.

He is so familiar with the aromas of the chocolate he uses, he knows so well how each couverture will express itself when transformed into a ganache, that you could say that the aromas live within him. Like a perfumer, he intuits the flavour associations, the interactions and harmonies between them. When preparing a ganache, he knows the dance the aromas will perform.

Jacques has given me a huge insight into the world of the bonbon. His are the only mint or ginger ganaches I will eat. I hated all ganaches made with tea (Earl Grey, Lapsong Souchong, Jasmine, and so forth) before meeting him. But with Jacques as the 'scientific genius', and in collaboration with tea taster and expert Lydia Gauthier, we created a line of 'tea ganaches' using teas no chocolatier had used so far. These treated both the tea and chocolate ingredients with respect, so that neither flavours were stifled.

Lydia suggested the teas, I proposed the chocolates to combine with each one, and Jacques experimented, changing tea concentrations and infusion times, and tailoring the proportions of different chocolates in the blend. Together we created a mini-range of three ganaches, far more exciting and palatable than the tea ganaches found in most chocolate shops. Our ganaches flavoured with 'Butterfly of Taiwan', 'Qimen Imperial' and 'Bancha Hojicha' were a novelty and a delight. They became part of Jacques' signature range – and are also included in the chocolate box offered to VIP guests at Alain Ducasse's hotels and restaurants.

TEA, COFFEE AND CHOCOLATE

Now you know about tea and chocolate – they *can* mix, when done well! But what about drinking tea while eating chocolate – or that favourite combination, coffee and chocolate?

I know many people love the two together, but I don't feel that either can be fully appreciated when they're mixed. The sugar in the chocolate (and worse if there is a fruit or alcohol flavouring) will hide the flavours of the coffee. What brings you pleasure when having chocolate with coffee is the sugar content of the chocolate. The aromas of the chocolate are drowned out by the coffee. Coffee kills the chocolate.

But having said this, I have been spotted eating chocolate and drinking tea at the same time... If you love to combine your chocolate with a hot drink, it's not the end of the world. But if you want to taste *all* the flavours, I suggest you savour your coffee and your chocolate singly, rather than together.

The art of the chocolatier

When making a bar, a chocolatier has to intuit which blends will work together, selecting couvertures to combine and working out the ideal proportions to use. If they just melt a readymade couverture (as many do), there's no need for talent or creativity.

A chocolatier making filled chocolates has to follow the same path as those making fine chocolate bars, but the task is even more complex. By now you know the wide variety of flavours found in chocolate: flowers, teas, alcohols, spices, fruits, nuts and more. But to create a filled chocolate you must think how the filling will taste with the coating. What flavour filling, what flavour coating?

Smelling different teas, a top chocolatier will suddenly feel inspired and think, 'Hmmm, this Qimen Imperial tea is nice, it will go better with dark than milk chocolate. The tea has clear leather notes in the attack and spicy notes at the end of the mouth. I will use a mix of the Valrhona chocolates Guanaja (classical, slightly masculine, elegant chocolate to carry the leather note) and Manjari (its acidity will enhance the shy, spicy notes of the tea)'.

A chocolatier must, of course, know his basic aromas (he will have a choco-database just as I do) and concentrate on creating the right combination in the right proportions, without looking at cost. His goal is to create a delight, a masterpiece. But there are limits. Not all combinations of flavour are possible in a filled chocolate.

Choosing the right couverture to go with each filling means having a good variety of couvertures to play with. Although you have seen the care that a good chocolatier will put into choosing the right chocolate to go with each filling, the reality is that few chocolatiers will bother. A lot of them, along with the manufacturers, use at the most one or two different chocolate couvertures as a basic ingredient to produce all their range – which means that they have only one or two aromatic palettes to work from. This is a great loss, as making superb chocolates is much more complex a matter than just putting milk chocolate with one range of fillings, and dark with another. And there is no guarantee that they have chosen good-quality couvertures or flavourings.

An etching of an eighteenth-century French artisanal chocolate shop

Becoming a chocolate connoisseur

And what about those fillings? A committed chocolatier views these as a fantastic journey into new worlds of aroma and flavour. Go into a chocolate shop and look at the filled chocolates counter, or open a pre-prepared box of chocolates. There's a whole world in there. But have the chocolates been made by a truly bold, creative chocolatier or one who copies others?

There are some basics that any chocolatier will have: plain ganaches, pralinés, marzipans. The creative ones usually have a wide range of combinations of flavours you are not used to seeing (and may not even have heard of!), such as Tonka beans or basil and lime ganaches. To see if a combination is pleasant, the only reliable way to test is to taste. Some combinations are really just marketing tools, used to cause interest (or horror): tobacco, cheese, or truffles for example!

Apart from looking at the range of fillings, though, how can you test the quality of a filled chocolate? Here is where my four-chocolate test comes into its own.

The four-chocolate test

When you find a new chocolatier, the ideal situation is to go into the shop armed with a list of questions. If you know what you want, this should prevent you from buying the wrong chocolates. Hunting down and selecting the right chocolates, the *best* chocolates, is far from a waste of time or money. When evaluating a chocolatier, you don't need to buy the whole range. A few carefully selected samples will tell you all you need to know about the entire range. Here are my tips...

Ask the person behind the counter to sell you one of each of the following. Use the exact words, to make sure that he or she understands that you know exactly what you want. (If the sales person doesn't know, ask for the chocolatier!) Don't accept any alternatives for this exercise. You will need:

1. **Ganaches.** A plain milk ganache (no alcohol whatsoever) and a plain dark ganache (no alcohol whatsoever).

2. **Marzipan.** A marzipan (not flavoured – ensure there is no pistachio or alcohol added – not even 'just a little bit'!).

3. **Pralinés.** A praliné (also not flavoured – you don't want chocolate added to the filling).

4. **Specialities.** Two of their house specialties or two chocolates they are proud of (they usually carry their logo).

Go home, and prepare to taste your chocolates alone and in the right tasting conditions (see Chapter 4)… as what follows is *not* sexy to look at!

When you are ready for the tasting, proceed as follows.

First, you need to find out the quality of the raw material used (mainly chocolate, but also the nut-based ingredients). This will help you to determine the quality of the chocolate maker's whole range.

1. The ganaches
The chocolate used to make the fillings is usually different from the one used for the coating. To start with, take a dark ganache (it's better to taste the one with less sugar first). Scrape the filling out of the chocolate coating. Keep the coating for later.

The ganache filling is the closest you can get to unadulterated chocolate. In a proper ganache, you shouldn't be able to taste the cream – it's just there to give it a smooth texture. If you can detect it, go back to the shop and ask for a fresher version (don't erase that chocolatier from your database just yet!). If the ganache is grainy, it means the chocolate maker failed to tame the ingredients. But again, be lenient. It happens to everybody at times. Go back to the shop and exchange it. If the texture is fine, move on.

Look at the ganache as you do when tasting a chocolate bar (see Chapter 4). Evaluate its texture and the aromatic palette (its notes and evolution over time). As you progress, you will eventually (as I do now) be able to recognise the chocolate used to make the ganache, even if it is a blend.

And what about the chocolate casing of the ganache? This is one more sign of the quality choices a chocolatier makes. In many cases, as I've said, all dark coatings are made with the same chocolate, and all milk coatings with the same milk chocolate. A coating has to be as neutral and fine as possible, so it doesn't 'pollute' the flavour you want to savour! Of course, the vast majority of chocolatiers cut costs on the coating, and use poor chocolate. Sniff the casing… and then taste it on its own. Do you detect sugar or vanillin? If not, you may be dealing with a quality chocolatier. The casing should be as good as the filling, as in the end, they mix in the mouth.

2. The praliné

Again, taste the filling first without the coating. Are the nuts good quality? Are they burned or rancid-tasting? Is it too sweet? (This is very common.) If you answer yes to any of these, it means the chocolatier went for cheap praliné ingredients. And now you know: the rest of the range has most probably been created with the same inattention to quality.

3. *The marzipan*

Is it juicy, slightly grainy and quartz-like (this is a good sign) or dry, crumbly and shiny white? A good marzipan is made with a ratio of sixty per cent nuts to forty per cent sugar, but the vast majority are actually more like forty per cent nuts to sixty per cent sugar. Can you taste the difference?

4. *The signature chocolates*

Even the chocolatiers we have leniently described here as *traditional* have at least one chocolate they designed and are very proud of. For any chocolatier in the French tradition, it is likely to be a plain ganache carrying their logo in gold. For others, it might be a revived traditional recipe.

Taste the chocolates, looking for creativity. If the chocolate is a simple combination of a standard good quality 70% blend with cream, for example, it will probably be good... but not exciting.

DISTINCTIVE SIGNATURE?

What are signature chocolates, exactly? Let's take Fortnum & Mason as an example, where the signature chocolates are the rose and violet creams, and the champagne and Bucks Fizz truffles.

The creams are produced exclusively for the shop with the finest natural essential oils. The exclusivity makes them signature chocolates. The truffles, on the other hand, have become signature chocolates because they are bestsellers.

Appalled by the alcoholic truffles (a serious no-no

to a connoisseur), I decided to create some more signature chocolates to try and make the selection a little more classy.

Fortnum & Mason's 'Finest Selection' comprises four plain truffles, two milk and two dark. They contain only cream and chocolate, no alcohol or preservatives, and the finest chocolate couvertures. Each one of the dark truffles is made with a different single-origin chocolate, Madagascar and Venezuela. The couvertures used have the same cocoa solids percentage, but a totally different aromatic palette. The two milk truffles are made with two fine and very different milk chocolates, creating two elegant ganaches, one with hints of fudge, and the other tasting of fresh full-fat milk.

The four-chocolate test is a great (and inexpensive) way to find out if you really want to commit yourself to a whole box of this chocolatier's range, and it will tell you whether the raw material your chocolatier is using is good enough to justify further investment.

Don't hesitate to complete your test with some questions. A good chocolatier is proud of his work, and will not hesitate to share with you which couvertures he uses, the story behind the name given to one of his chocolates, or the choice of a flavouring. Give him a few hints of your move into the world of chocolate, and, if the queue is not too long, the frankness of his answers and the quality of the time devoted to your conversation should give you an indicator of whether he is a businessman or an artist.

Finding your way around the chocolate shop

Perhaps you're a regular visitor already, buying up lots of filled chocolates. Or maybe you decide that it's finally time to pull open the heavy glass doors and step into the hushed interior of a chocolate shop you've never visited. Wherever you're coming from, you now know what to ask for on your first visit and how to taste what you've bought.

But of course there's a lot more on offer than just the few chocolates on your checklist. For example, if you come into Fortnum & Mason, you'll find the chocolates grouped by categories: nutty (plain chocolate and nuts), creams, marzipans, alcohol ganaches, fruity ganaches, pralinés, and Swiss, French and Belgian chocolates in separate cases – as often customers have a preference for one country's choco-tradition.

If you want to buy more than just the ones I've recommended to start with, here are a few of my favourite fruit and nut combinations – a delightful and healthy complement to chocolate bars.

- Milk chocolate with hazelnuts

- Dark chocolate and almonds

- Orange and dark chocolate

- Lemon and milk chocolate

- Candied ginger marries well with either milk or dark chocolate – but only when it is made with fine ingredients.

Any other fruit pollutes the chocolate taste, in my opinion.

And what if you have been given a box of chocolates? Or what if your box doesn't have a menu? Well, you can do a blind taste test – you don't need to be told what the flavours are! Use the methodology outlined above. You might find that they're not all to your taste, though. Sadly, people tend not to give me boxes of chocolates as a gift – nobody is brave enough to buy for a professional chocolate buyer! A pity – as I love to discover new creations. On the bright side, though, a connoisseur will generally know what they want, and once you know your way around filled chocolates a little more, you'll be able to walk into a chocolate shop, look around, and know exactly what suits you best, just as I do.

Truffles

MAKES ABOUT 4 DOZEN TRUFFLES

As you can now buy fine chocolate couverture, you can make your own divine truffles, and present them attractively in gift boxes for your friends. This recipe comes from Cyril Prudhomme, a talented chocolatier I worked with at Ladurée in Paris.

20 ounces Valrhona Caraque chocolate couverture,
or other fine chocolate
10 ounces Valrhona Caraïbe chocolate couverture,
or other fine chocolate
2 cups light cream
¼ cup honey
1 vanilla bean, split open
2 tablespoons good-quality unsalted butter, diced
cocoa powder (the best you can find, such as
Valrhona or Scharffen Berger)

1. Finely chop the chocolate and put it in a bowl large enough to hold all the other ingredients, too.

2. Bring the cream, honey and the vanilla bean to a boil in a saucepan over medium heat. Remove the vanilla bean; pour the hot cream mixture, one-third at a time, over the chocolate, whisking each time to incorporate (but avoid getting air into the mixture). An elastic texture and shine show the chocolate mixture is ready. (Alternatively, place the chocolate in a blender and pour all the hot cream mixture over the chocolate and mix for 3 minutes.)

3. When the chocolate mixture is 95–104° F, blend in the butter.

4. Let cool to 72–75°F. Whisk the mixture lightly to add a little air, mold into about 1½-inch balls, chill until firm, and coat with cocoa powder. Eat immediately!

Note: The truffles can be refrigerated for three to four days, but for the best flavor, bring them to room temperature before eating.

Whether you stick to your beloved filled chocolates or prefer bars, the most important thing is to use the tips in this book to hunt for the best quality within your own preferences. This will mean that you'll have to look for the chocolatiers using fine ingredients and, consequently, will have to pay more than in the past – but believe me, the pleasure will be a concentrated one!

CHAPTER 8

·

Chocolate: friend or foe?

THE TASTING EXERCISES in Chapter 4 may have come easily to you. But if they didn't, one obstacle may have been the way that you think about chocolate. Is it your friend, or your enemy? Is it good for you, or bad? Do you love eating it, but hate yourself when you do so? Most people have mixed feelings about chocolate.

When I run chocolate tasting workshops, I always ask people about the feelings and thoughts they associate with it.

They love it, that's for sure. It makes them feel good because of the happy memories it nearly always revives (plus it contains chemicals that boost your happiness quota – see pages 165–7).

But it also makes them feel guilty, and bad – and that's because of the many myths and misunderstandings about chocolate that have built up over generations and still abound. Luckily, most of these are untrue. In this chapter I will help you to look at your own emotional relationship with chocolate and discover what is holding you back from becoming a connoisseur – and what you can do about it.

Chocolate on the couch...

If I asked you to close your eyes and imagine yourself biting into a piece of chocolate, your mind would immediately conjure up a bar with which you are already very familiar – and, as you love chocolate, the one you think of is bound to be a personal favourite. You can smell it, taste it, feel it in your mouth. You can even experience the warm sensations it will bring as you savour it, the aftertaste it will leave – and, more than likely, that awful sense of guilt after you've eaten it.

This simple exercise reveals a lot about the psychological obstacles that may be holding you back in your chocolate education. Firstly, you already have your favourite chocolates – your mind is made up about what chocolate should taste like. Secondly, you have preconceptions about chocolate that make you feel guilty when you eat it – usually that it is an indulgence that you don't deserve (because of cost, frivolity, calories, or the fact that it's a reward you haven't 'earned').

When I offer someone a new chocolate to try, I can tell immediately from their reaction whether they are weighed down with psychological baggage – associations they need to dump – or whether they are openminded, receptive and adventurous: ready to try something new.

Before any of us can move on, we have to understand why we feel the way we do about our chocolate, and much of this is to do with what psychologists call 'cultural references'. In the same way that we learn language and idiosyncrasies of dialect and vocabulary – according to where we were raised and by whom, and who we have mixed with as we've grown up – it is the influence of family and friends that leads us towards certain types of chocolate. This influence is so strong that whole nations have specific chocolate preferences.

In Chapter 1 I listed the favourite tastes of Europeans – mostly sweetened milk chocolate (except the French).

We like it because it's become traditional and it's the chocolate to which we are introduced at a very young age, but we are also biologically programmed to like this kind of chocolate. As babies our first food is our mother's milk (or a formula imitation) – which is fatty and slightly sweet. Most mass-market chocolate is also a combination of fat and sugar. So falling in love with it as a child couldn't come more naturally!

If, as you have matured, you have developed a more savoury palate, and are no longer so attracted to sweet chocolate, moving on from these early chocolate associations will come easily. If you have a sweet tooth, it's going to be harder – but a dark chocolate that's packed with flavours will take your mind off its lack of sugar and milky mildness.

On top of simply liking a certain type of chocolate are your own memories. So recognising that you like what you like 'because it's the chocolate I've always eaten', or 'it's the taste I associate with rewards – and it makes me feel good about myself' can help you to put these thoughts aside, in an imaginary locked box, while you get on with the job of tasting something new.

But there are still those feelings of guilt to tackle.

Take a moment to think about the three main thoughts you immediately associate with chocolate and write them down. For example, 'it gives you spots', 'it makes you fat', 'it's naughty but nice!' Now add another seven common beliefs about chocolate. For example, 'it's unhealthy', 'it's an aphro-disiac', 'it causes cravings', 'it causes mood swings', 'it's bad for your teeth', 'it's addictive', 'it's high in caffeine'. (Of course, you may have other ideas for your list.) Now write down the four main reasons you feel guilty when you have chocolate. Why does it make you feel so bad about yourself?

Some of the thoughts on your list have probably suggested chocolate is sinful in some way. It's nothing new – chocolate has always been controversial. Back in Chapter 1 we saw how the Spanish women of St Cristobal de las Casas were banned from drinking hot chocolate during high mass. But then, between 1650 and the late 1860s, it was recommended by doctors and pharmacologists as a health aid. Today the controversy rages on. We have people telling us it's healthy, and others telling us it's bad for us.

The media would not have to keep repeating the message that 'chocolate is good for health' if we weren't so severely handicapped by the myths that surround it. These myths are a major obstacle to becoming a connoisseur, as they present themselves as soon as you start to bite into a chocolate – and this actually 'pollutes' the palate with enzymes.

Close your eyes and remember the last time you had a chocolate for pleasure. Guilt probably flashed through your head as you bought the chocolate, possessed you as you took your first bite, and reminded you, while you were trying to enjoy your mouthful, that you were 'sinning'. Guilt spoils any sensual delight you hoped to derive, and normally gets worse when you have swallowed the chocolate – leaving you with just guilt and no physical pleasure.

We perpetuate these beliefs about chocolate by passing them from one generation to the next. From an early age our parents teach us not to eat too much chocolate, and to ask permission before helping ourselves to it. But they also use it as a reward, or a carrot to entice us to behave ourselves or do our chores… It is even the first culprit called to blame when, as children, we feel sick or have a headache ('You shouldn't have eaten so much chocolate!'). As a result, chocolate becomes a forbidden food, and something children are bound to try to sneak from the kitchen. I guess I was born to become a connoisseur as I had a quite exceptional mother who praised the yummy properties of chocolate – and she was the one who stole my precious stock!

DID YOU KNOW?

It is impossible to taste chocolate properly when negative thoughts about it are lurking in your mind. These negative thoughts provoke the secretion of enzymes that cause an acid environment in your mouth, so your taste buds will not be neutral and ready for analysis. Any conclusion you reach will be inaccurate. You may even eliminate from your choco database one that would have been worthy of your survival kit!

But what about all those myths – the spots, the weight gain, the dental rot? If we are talking about 'vegelate' – fat, sugar and flavouring – all those health risks may well be true. But real chocolate does not harm your health. Just look at the evidence … (and remember, we are talking about pure dark chocolate bars, not your fancy truffles or favourite milk bar!).

- **It's good for your health**

Back in the sixteenth century, the Spanish, who were as obsessed with health and diet as we are today, regarded chocolate as a health food. Chocolate bars are good for you – and here's why:

Chocolate fat is not all bad!

Cocoa butter – the fat that occurs naturally in cocoa beans – contains a lot of fat. The good news is that it is 'good' fat, as is found in olive oil. Typically, there's 1½ oz of fat in a 3½ oz 72% bar of dark chocolate. Of this, ¼ oz will be saturated fat. But the ⅓ oz of unsaturated fat are composed of oleic acid, which raises HDL cholesterol (the type that helps to protect your heart) and lowers levels of unhealthy LDL cholesterol. Of the saturated fat, more than half is composed of stearic acid, a fatty acid that is converted by the liver to more healthy oleic acid.

And, although a quarter of the fat in chocolate is palmitic acid – the dominant fatty acid in beef, pork, and dairy (and the fat believed to be most culpable in raising cholesterol levels and contributing to atherosclerosis) – studies show that the good chocolate fats largely counteract the bad, having a positive effect on cholesterol.

It's packed with minerals

It's true! A 3½ oz dark chocolate bar provides the following percentages of your daily mineral requirements:

Iron 20%   Phosphorous 30%
Magnesium 33%   Copper 25%
Potassium 27%   Calcium 13%.

It's a major source of antioxidants

In a US Department of Agriculture list of high-antioxidant foods, dark chocolate actually comes out on top – with 13,120 ORAC (Oxygen Radical Absorbance Capacity) units, nearly twice the antioxidants in milk chocolate, and more than double the ORAC units in the next best thing, the humble prune! These antioxidants are like a troop of bomb disposal experts, whose job it is to diffuse the free radicals that cause premature ageing and destruction in the body's cells.

Not only does chocolate contain high concentrations of antioxidants, it contains the highest quality of the lot – the same flavonoids (polyphenol antioxidants that are 100 times stronger than vitamin C) as red wine and green tea (credited with reducing heart attack risk and cancer), of which one, proanthocyanidin, is one of the few compounds that can cross the blood-brain barrier to protect brain tissue. The same compound also blocks the formation of enzymes in the body that cause inflammation and arthritis; and it acts as an antihistamine to protect against allergies.

A cup of hot cocoa (made with cocoa powder) has twice as many healthy antioxidants as a glass of red wine, and four times more than a cup of green tea, according to a study at Cornell University in 2003!

Of course, the health bandwagon is another useful marketing tool for big companies who want to promote chocolate (but may yet be uninterested in quality). A major brand has started to promote a new chocolate, even higher in antioxidants than normal chocolate. Is it worth it? Well, I would never suggest that chocolate should be your *only* source of antioxidants, so there's no need to sacrifice flavour for health. As I've said before, chocolate should be about pleasure!

- **It's good for your teeth**

Dental decay is caused by bacteria which accumulate in plaque on the surface of your teeth, especially in the absence of good oral hygiene. Chocolate, because of the sugar it contains, has long been associated with tooth decay in the minds of the public and some dentists. But studies show no direct evidence of a significant link. If anything, chocolate is *good* for your teeth, as cocoa contains fluoride, and the cocoa butter forms a coating in the teeth that protects against bacteria. However, the sweeter the chocolate, the less this is the case.

- **It doesn't give you acne**

The cause of acne is unknown, but contributory factors include hormonal changes around puberty and changes in the skin's bacterial status. No study has so far demonstrated a link between chocolate and acne, even though this link is often made. If a liking for cheap chocolate is accompanied by spots, it may more accurately be a sign that you are not taking care of your diet generally. For example, you may be eating too much junk food and not enough fresh fruit and vegetables.

- **It doesn't make you fat** (unless you want it to)

Having eaten more than a pound of chocolate a day for the last 15 years and still managing to maintain a weight of 100 to 105 lbs for my height of 5 ft 3 in, I am living proof of this. There are a few rules, however:

- It helps if you can try to eat chocolate on its own – not mixed with other foods. Give it a go, and you'll realise that your taste buds are more sensitive away from mealtimes. You should be able to derive a more intense pleasure from the chocolate, making it also easier not to overeat.

- You should also try to keep active. You put on weight when you consume more calories than you burn. I am a very sporty person. I sleep fewer than six hours a night and have been swimming for an hour a day over the last 20 years. This is also why I can get away with eating so much chocolate daily.

- Listen to your body. Try to tune into the right chocolate for your mood. Once you learn to find the chocolate that best fits your mood or moment, your body will also tell you when to stop. Of course, the larger your chocolate database, the finer-tuned you'll be to what you need. The danger, if you eat chocolate that is too sweet, is that the sugar will inhibit this internal regulator and trigger a demand for 'more'. Sugar is the evil in chocolate.

• It boosts the 'feelgood' factor

Have you ever tried this trick? Your post arrives in the morning, and you can see that there's an envelope you've been expecting. It contains the results of a recent job interview or a bank statement. You know it could be bad news. How can you make it less bad? By eating half a bar of chocolate before you open it! Of course it won't change the content of the letter… But it will change the way you react to the news, even if it isn't good.

Whenever I face a difficult moment, or bad news, I eat half a bar of chocolate. It has been scientifically proven that chocolate makes you feel good – or at least less bad.

Chocolate contains many psychoactive molecules which all contribute to making you feel better. It elevates your mood, reduces anxiety, and is probably the world's most pleasant antidepressant!

- Chocolate contains caffeine and theobromine, which stimulate the brain and central nervous system, giving you a burst of energy.

- Chocolate also contains phenylethylamine (PEA), a close relative to amphetamines, which increases attention and activity. PEA has also been shown to relieve depression. You get a surge of PEA when you fall in love, and it floods your brain during orgasm!

- Two other pleasure substances are also to be found in chocolate – N-oleoylethanolamine and N-linoleylethanolamine – which have a make-up similar to the brain's pleasure chemical anandamide ('ananda' is the Sanskrit for 'bliss').

If this all sounds very scientific, let me explain. Imagine someone gives you a lovely box of chocolates (in my case, please fill it with a selection of plain dark chocolate bars!). Your brain interprets this action as 'someone cares for me'. This pleasant news triggers the production of natural endorphins – feel-good chemicals – in the brain. It is a beautiful box (the aesthetic pleasure triggers more endorphins); and the delicious-smelling chocolates instantly remind you of past sensual chocolate experiences (your mouth salivates and your brain produces yet more feel-good chemicals). When you finally eat a chocolate (containing phenylethylamine), your pleasure is maximised. You are high on chocolate.

So beyond the delightful experience of actually eating it, chocolate is also an elixir for mental well-being.

BUT IS IT AN APHRODISIAC?

Well, let's see... I've just told you how much chocolate I get through on a daily basis. How could I manage to hold down my job as manager in a traditional company if all that chocolate was firing up my sex drive? I'd be wearing lowcut dresses, baring my legs, trying to seduce my colleagues...

Seriously, the chocolate aphrodisiac myth is one that people like to maintain. It's a fantasy – albeit one with rather a lot of history behind it. The Aztec emperor Moctezuma is thought to have drunk 50 golden goblets of chocolate a day, allegedly to enhance his sexual prowess. So when chocolate was discovered by the Spanish conquistadors and introduced to Europe, it was natural for the Spanish and eventually the rest of the world to associate it with love.

The reasons for this can also be seen in the effects of chocolate on human behaviour. As I mentioned earlier, chocolate contains the same mood-lifting chemicals that rush in when we are experiencing feelings of love or lust. Chocolate also gives an immediate and substantial energy boost, thus increasing stamina. And although that could be credited with having boosted Casanova's sexual prowess (and he is said to have consumed chocolate as an aphrodisiac before frolicking with his conquests), recent

research suggests that women are actually more sus-
ceptible to the effects of phenylethylamine than men.
Casanova obviously didn't know this, as there's no
mention of him sharing his chocolate with the ladies.
Perhaps he thought his charms alone were enough to
guarantee success!

We turn to chocolate for comfort, but is it really any substitute for affection?

I like to quote the humorist Sandra Boynton on this topic.
She says:

> Clearly it is not the lovelorn sufferer who seeks solace in
> chocolate, but rather the chocolate-deprived individual
> who, desperate, seeks in mere love a pale approximation
> of bittersweet euphoria.

• It won't give you a migraine

Twenty to 75 per cent of migraine sufferers associate chocolate with migraine, although few actively avoid it. As I understand it, chocolate is implicated as a trigger only in less than
five per cent of cases. While some headaches are partly
chocolate-induced, probably related to chemicals such as
phenylethylamine, headache-inducing chemicals are also
found in aged cheeses, processed meat, coffee, peanuts and
red wine. It is the accumulation of various triggers that provoke headache, and only in people predisposed to regular
headaches. I really don't think poor chocolate should carry
all the responsibility.

• Its stimulants are no bad thing

Chocolate contains two stimulants: caffeine and theobromine. Theobromine's effects on the body resemble those of caffeine.

We all know that coffee, tea and cola contain caffeine. And we all hear that 'caffeine is bad for you'. But in actuality, a small intake of caffeine has positive benefits: it increases vigilance, and delays the symptoms of tiredness. A cup of coffee a day will not harm you, but like any food, and like anything in life, it becomes harmful if you have too much of it. The good news is that the caffeine content in chocolate is negligible. A teaspoon of cocoa powder carries 6mg of caffeine and a 1½ oz bar of dark chocolate carries 28 mg. Compare this to coffee and colas: a regular coffee (8½ oz) carries 65 to 150mg, and a 12 oz cola carries 40 to 50mg. So you would need to eat 3½ oz of dark chocolate – two and a half 1½ oz bars – all at once to have the caffeine effect of a regular cup of coffee.

Theobromine is found in the greatest quantities in chocolate; in fact, there is four times more theobromine than caffeine in chocolate. Luckily, theobromine is good for you: it stimulates the nervous system and boosts muscle performance.

• It doesn't cause cravings

When we get angry that we haven't managed to resist a chocolate, is it the chocolate's fault? I think 'chocolate' cravings are actually more often than not sugar cravings, resulting from the high sugar content in cheaper chocolates. Chocolate is so much more attractive than any cake, biscuit or sweet: it is scientifically proven to contain the ideal combination of fat and sugar. It is one of life's greatest pleasures.

Chocolate cravings have three main causes, and they are to do with us – not the chocolate, so they are something we can learn to control.

1. Chocolate is seen as a 'forbidden food'. A study at the University of Sussex in England looked at the effects of chocolate as a forbidden food, using a group of 30 women who were at their normal weight. Half the group were allowed free access to chocolate; the other half were told it was forbidden. After 24 hours, the latter group was allowed to eat as much of it as they wanted – and ate much more compared with those who had been allowed chocolate all along.

The message is clear. When we think of chocolate as a forbidden food, it becomes more tempting, and we are more likely to eat too much of it. The messages we have grown up with – chocolate is bad for you, it should be restricted, and so on, and those we impose on ourselves when we try to diet or curb chocolate consumption for some other reason – are the ones that are ironically causing us to eat more of it, and to crave it.

As you become a connoisseur, this kind of craving will be less of a problem. Chocolate will no longer frighten you. Once you understand your choco-psyche and discover quality chocolate, you'll instinctively eat more slowly and selectively. I believe if you listen to your body and reward it with what it asks for, you'll not only enjoy the chocolate more, but will actually eat less of it.

2. Chocolate is 'moreish'. The desire to eat more occurs during rather than preceding the eating episode, and it can apply to any food you enjoy. It is most often experienced when you attempt to limit how much you will eat before your appetite is sated. Sugar is the main culprit behind the call for 'more'. As you begin to explore chocolate, trying darker and less sugar-laden varieties, you'll be less likely to become a victim of moreishness!

3. Cravings are often related to changes in mood. They affect the way we eat chocolate, but also the way we speak to other people, how well we concentrate, and so on. Premenstrual changes are often linked with chocolate cravings, but these have more to do with the sufferer's personal makeup (her sensuality, emotions and social values) than to the psychoactive chemicals contained in chocolate.

• It is not addictive

The word 'chocoholic' is often used to describe people who eat a lot of chocolate. I personally dislike this word: it's too close to alcoholic, and maintains the myth that chocolate is addictive. Which it is not. Addiction is generally associated with drug and alcohol abuse, or compulsive sexual activity. It's true that for some people, eating chocolate is a compulsive behaviour, but for people without disordered eating patterns, stopping the consumption of chocolate simply causes displeasure – not withdrawal symptoms.

In 1994, Professor Chantal Fabre-Bismuth, a specialist in toxicology, conducted a study at the hospital Fernand Vidal in Paris. She analysed the quantities and pattern of intake of 40 people eating more than 3½ oz chocolate per day (she had not met me!). The results showed that when the participants were deprived of chocolate, there were no withdrawal symptoms, they were just… less happy! They simply missed the pleasure. In no way were their physical and mental capacities affected.

> Despite the amount of chocolate I eat, I do not qualify myself as a chocoholic, at all. I am a choco-gourmet. I enjoy good chocolate more than anything else on earth, and I am also an epicurean. I eat a lot of chocolate. But you can lock me for days in a room full of poor-quality chocolate, *of any percentage*, and I'd rather starve. As you become a chocolate connoisseur, you will understand what I mean here. You will be able to look at some chocolate displays in shops or in a box proffered to you with total calm and control – even nausea in some cases.

But… and this is very important: remember that all the beneficial properties I've outlined above apply *only* to chocolate bars made of real chocolate with at least 60% cocoa content. Poor-quality, low-cocoa chocolate does not count. Beware of the following:

• Too much sugar

If you crave sweet milk chocolate, it's the sugar you are craving, not the chocolate: it will confuse your palate, and lead you to eat more than you need. And this is a big stumbling block for chocolate lovers who want to maintain a healthy weight. Don't try to cut down on the calories by going for so-called sugar-free chocolate (unless you really are diabetic). These bars are made with maltitol instead of sugar, and as this is a chemical sweetener, it brings its own chemical flavours and it is still moreish. Your chocolate not only tastes bad (or worse, depending on your starting point), but it is still calorific, at 450 calories per 3½ oz – if you eat the whole bar. So unless you're a masochist or diabetic, ban all sugar-free bars from sight!

• White chocolate

I don't have much regard for this. White chocolate is made with cocoa butter, but contains no actual cocoa mass. In my opinion, it's about as tasty as eating a piece of paper coated with sugar and milk powder!

• Carob

Carob, also known as St John's bread, algarroba, locust bean and locust pod, is used by some as a substitute for chocolate. It has some similar nutrients (calcium and phosphorous) and, when combined with vegetable fat and sugar, it can be made to approximate the colour and consistency of chocolate. Of course, as writer and chocolate-lover Sandra Boynton puts it: 'The same arguments can persuasively be made in favour of dirt.'

• Price

There's no way round this: quality chocolate is more expensive than the cheap varieties – but so is luxurious wrapping. Don't be taken in by manufacturers who care more about the quality of their paper, boxes, gold lettering and ribbons than that of their raw materials!

- ## Percentage

People who say they only eat 70% cocoa chocolate need to realise that percentage is only part of the story. A high-alcohol wine is not necessarily better than a low-alcohol one. Nobody would judge a wine on its alcohol content. What matters is its bouquet of aromas, its symphony of flavours. In other words, it's all down to quality of ingredients and manufacture, *not* cocoa percentage all on its own.

Having said this, though, the higher the percentage of cocoa, the less sugar the bar will have. And the less milk powder a bar contains, the less fatty that bar will be. So there is a case for sticking to dark chocolate if you are concerned about eating too much sugar or fat.

And finally…

To start thinking like a connoisseur, you need to be open-minded, able to take what other people say about chocolate with a sceptical pinch of salt. You need to re-evaluate what chocolate means to *you*, forget all that you have thought about it to date (it is not something to feel guilty and bad about, it is to be enjoyed and esteemed!), and start with a fresh mind, a clean palate and a new page in your tasting notebook. You need to know that you can confidently eat chocolate without the fear that it will give you a headache, spots or excess weight. All these things will become possible, and, in the next chapter, I will show you how becoming a connoisseur can change your life – and even your career.

CHAPTER 9

·

Becoming a connoisseur

*I*F CHOCOLATE IS YOUR passion, then a job that pays you to taste chocolate for a living must seem like heaven on earth. Such jobs are, of course, few and far between. But it may amaze you to learn that you do not necessarily have to be a professional chocolate worker to achieve such dizzy heights.

At the time that I applied for my job as chocolate buyer for Fortnum & Mason, I was working for the cosmetics company L'Oréal – and the bulk of my chocolate career had so far been amateur rather than professional.

As I've said, I had qualified as an agronomist. But alongside the scientific studies, I had, as you've seen, been secretly studying chocolate for years. I would taste it and make notes on it, sampling everything I could in the growing quality market. When I left my job at the UN in Jamaica, I decided I wanted a complete change from all that – and that's when I wrote off to the chocolate companies, offering my services for free in order to learn more about chocolate. And as you know, it was Ladurée, the Paris chocolate shop, that finally gave me a chance.

I really have worked my way up from the bottom. I started on the production line, wearing a white gown and hat and doing everything from putting the delicious ingredients into the mixer to packing the finished chocolates into boxes.

During my first few days, I was putting a lot in my mouth along the way and the production manager said loudly, 'You will soon get tired of it – everyone does.' Four days later, he told our boss, chocolatier Pierre Hermé, 'In 18 years, I have never seen that!' I put another chocolate in my mouth, smiling at M. Hermé, my eyes sparkling with delight. He just laughed, knowing that he had met a true chocophile. By the end of my time at Ladurée I was managing the confectionary department.

However, that job would not have been enough to get me a look-in at Fortnum & Mason had the position been advertised when I was still at Ladurée. Ultimately, I believe, I got the job because of my passion for chocolate. After leaving Ladurée, I spent three years at L'Oréal, but continued to chisel away at the chocolate world in all my spare time – evenings, weekends, holidays. I founded a chocolate association in 1999 (Carrément Chocolat) and presented at chocolate conferences, gave tasting courses, and hosted special chocolate evenings for major companies. I was thirsty for knowledge and attended every chocolate conference or show I could, and visited as many factories and plantations as possible. Although it could be tiring, I was truly living my passion.

One day in August 2002, I switched on my computer to find 23 emails from friends, who had all seen a particular job advertisement. It went something like this:

CHOCOLATE BUYER

Are you looking for the best job in the world? Well, here it is! What could be better than being the Chocolate Buyer at Fortnum & Mason's world-renowned Food Hall?

Do you think you have what it takes to be this unique and innovative individual, able to inspire others with your passion for chocolate?

If you are this person then tell us why you believe that you can make a difference. We are looking for enthusiasm, creative flair and energy to develop the already divine range of products available.

Nearly every one of those 23 emails said, 'You were born for this'! And by this time, thanks to my extracurricular interests in the chocolate world, I had amassed enough experience to give me a decent chocolate-oriented CV – even though I had never attended a cooking or chocolate school. I sent my CV to Fortnum & Mason and was selected from a field of 3,000 – a turning point in my choco-life!

A day in the life of a chocolate connoisseur

People are always fascinated to know how a chocoholic who works with chocolate spends her day… 'So, do you really eat chocolate all day long?' my suppliers ask. Well, I didn't need the excuse of working in the chocolate business to start eating a pound of it a day – I've been doing that for long enough. But, yes, it is true… I do spend the day eating chocolate! Some for work, most for pleasure.

5 am: My stereo wakes me up with classical music. I stay in bed, eyes closed, enjoying the music.

5:15 am: Brush my teeth and prepare the tasting tray. I will wait until 45 minutes after brushing my teeth as the toothpaste would otherwise still be polluting my taste buds. I have normally decided on the theme of my tasting the night before, and a box of samples (many from suppliers wanting me to buy their chocolate for Fortnum & Mason) is waiting in the kitchen. (The rest of my personal chocolate stock is stored in a special cool, dark room.)

6.00 am: I have my first chocolate tasting of the day! This is the best time, when my palate is completely clean and fully receptive to the aromas and flavours I am about to encounter.

6.45 am: I head for the local swimming pool, where I swim for an hour a day nonstop (around 1¼ mi). Exercise is absolutely essential if you eat a lot of chocolate! The chocolate I eat provides an entire day's worth of calories, so swimming helps to make room for the other foods I need. I also do a lot of brisk walking and power yoga. Just as with listening (really listening!) to good music, these activities give me a sense of well-being, a harmony between body and mind, which I find essential. It helps me to eliminate any mental 'chatter' and listen fully to my senses while tasting.

8.40 am: Back on the Tube for the 20-minute journey to work. I take this opportunity to catch up on any chocolate-related reading.

9.00 am: I arrive at Fortnum & Mason and go straight to the shop floor to pick myself an assortment of chocolate. The filled chocolates I like are mainly nuts with chocolate (hazelnut or almond bâtonnets in chocolate, the nutty pralinés, lemon peel in milk chocolate (one I introduced to Fortnum & Mason), a plain dark truffle using beans from Madagascar. Then I select three plain dark chocolate bars (generally two favourites, and one more that I want to rediscover). My morning kit weighs 12¼ oz, the bars represent 8 oz of it – and it will be usually be finished by lunchtime at 2 pm. I spit out everything I taste.

You're probably thinking, 'That's a *lot* of chocolate'! Well, it is, but I have to thank my taste buds for having a natural inclination towards nutty fillings rather than creamy ones. They're much less fattening, and the dark chocolate with nuts combination is actually pretty healthy. And, of course, ganaches are far more fattening than bars or pralinés.

9.15 am: I have breakfast at my desk as I check my work emails. If I start eating chocolate now, it will become an exclusively chocolate breakfast as I never mix chocolate with any other food – and I try not to do this more than twice a week. My regular breakfast is either fruit or a plain full-fat (full flavour!) yogurt.

9.30 am: The first phone call of the day from a potential supplier. 'My name is X. Our company sells outstanding confectionary products and I would be grateful if you could make some time to meet me...'

My response is standard. 'Thank you for your call, X; however, I would love to meet your chocolates first and I will leave it to my palate to decide if we shall meet. Please could you send me samples with the prices, shelf-life, ingredients list and availability over the year? I also need to know how long you take to deliver, who else in the UK sells your chocolate; and I would ask you to label your samples so that I know in advance what they are. Please also package those with alcohol separately.'

By then they usually say that they would like to see my reaction as I taste their wonderful chocolate.

'I totally understand and respect that. However, I taste at 6 am at home. If you wish to leave me your telephone number I will let you know when I plan to do the tasting and you may join me.'

Unsurprisingly, I haven't yet had a supplier take me up on this... and in fact, no one has even got as far as asking for my address!

10 am: I am called to the shop floor. A couple of Dutch tourists are looking for a bar I have never heard of, so I get them to describe it, then show them a few products I think they will find very similar. I also take the opportunity of introducing them to our range of plantation and single-origin bars. I know my eyes must be twinkling because I am very proud of this range, which is unique in the UK.

I have excited their curiosity and they decide to buy a set of four different bars. These two people make my day. I have somehow 'brought the choco-light' to them – it's a small thing, but, brick by brick, one can slowly construct a temple.

When I visit the chocolate counter, I watch the way customers select the chocolates and if I see any hesitation, I propose my assistance. Whether they are buying for themselves or as a present, I see it as an opportunity for them to discover a few different chocolates, close to those they like and are used to, but a step closer to the temple of fine chocolate!

10.30 am: Next, I systematically look at the filled chocolates in the fridges, spotting bloomed or damaged ones, which I then have removed. A bloomed chocolate, which looks grey or dull, has suffered from a too-fast change of temperature and humidity. It will still taste good but aesthetics are part of the pleasure, and in one of the finest department stores in the world, everything needs to be perfect.

Happily, there's no need for these chocolates to go to waste. Any bloomed chocolates go to the staff canteen – I love to see people's faces illuminated as they see the chocolates on offer. I feel like Father Christmas!

10.40 am: Back at my desk, my selection of chocolates by my side, I try to focus on the pile of paperwork – correspondence, orders, and complaints. When I bring a new product in – to refresh the range or to upgrade quality –I have to take one out to make space, and I then get letters from customers surprised and disappointed about the change. It is hard to please everybody, and I just hope that they will one day try one of the new ones.

11.30 am: We have a meeting to select the products we will present in the Christmas catalogue. This has to be started at least ten months ahead of Christmas.

2 pm: Lunch. After lunch, usually salad and a sandwich, I will not eat chocolate for at least two hours (or up to four if I have been taken out for a heavy lunch). If I do feel the urge, I go for a bite of Michael Recchiuti's 85% – I find this high-cocoa, good-quality bar the only pleasant chocolate to eat after a meal. Even 75% cocoa chocolate seems too sugary, and not sufficiently chocolatey, eaten close to a meal. Most of the time I go for cocoa nibs, though, which are perfect when you are not feeling like sweets but want to taste something that stirs your senses.

2:30 pm: Meeting with my assistant. We share information and tasks, and decide on products we wish to carry as Christmas novelties.

3.30 pm: I receive a call from the Italian chamber of commerce. I am invited to spend three days in Turin for their big annual chocolate show. I will have a series of meetings with the little-known small business confectioners who make Italy's best little chocolate jewels. I immediately make two more phone calls. One to book my flight, and the other to Domori, whose factory in Italy makes astonishingly expensive chocolate. This makes liking their bars a pricey pleasure, but I am nevertheless amazed by them, as they trigger a new set of feelings in my mouth.

Domori's brochures are so sophisticated and complete (they even created a chocolate quality code – which they have to stick to!) that I want to know more about the company. Furthermore, competitors tell me Domori don't work from the bean (which means they are buying their cocoa mass from another company, and just melt, blend, temper and mould). I am intrigued by this, because the chocolate tastes like no other I have tried, and I want to see with my own eyes what they are doing. Working for Fortnum & Mason opens almost all doors to me, and allows me to deepen my knowledge and the scope of sharing it.

5 pm: I feel like having a chocolate that's not in my box, so I pop down to the storeroom and examine the boxes. Hmmm. A good opportunity to check all the sell-by dates and stock levels. I remove any box whose shelf-life is too short to be sold – I need to make sure it doesn't accidentally end up on the shop floor.

6 pm: My assistant and I make a comparative tasting of raw materials such as candied ginger or orange. Improving our range also means encouraging the companies that produce Fortnum & Mason-branded chocolates to improve the quality of their raw material. I then negotiate prices and organise a delivery at their production unit – ensuring that everything goes according to plan.

6.30 pm: At the end of the working day, I will go to a yoga class, then return home to eat dinner, relax by listening to music, and then catch up with emails from my friends in the worlds of chocolate, perfume, tea and coffee, eager to get updated on the fight for quality elsewhere in the world.

What does it take?

Anyone can eat and enjoy chocolate, but you have to go the extra mile to develop your knowledge if you want to be taken seriously in the chocolate world.

- Acquaint yourself with chocolate, tasting every new bar on the market (but stick to the quality market – forget anything else!).

- Develop your own chocolate database, noting aromas, flavours and textures of new bars. Go back to Chapters 2 and 4 to find out more about how you should do this.

- Attend chocolate events – there are annual chocolate shows in London, Paris, New York, San Francisco, Tokyo, and even in Russia now! Here you will meet the names behind the bars, and pick up all the news that only chocolate insiders are normally privy to.

- Join chocolate clubs, attend their meetings if possible, read the reviews on their websites, and hunt for tips and addresses. Write your own reviews on the website forums, but don't be influenced too much by what others say. Your own opinion is all you need, but these forums are valuable for information and ideas.

- Get some practical knowledge, too – is there anywhere where you could work alongside a chocolatier for free in order to gain more experience? You can also attend specialised chocolate courses. They exist in most cities of a reasonable size, and usually are a week long.

When you start to make a name for yourself in any area – perhaps by writing articles on the subject, or hosting workshops (even if you have to invite an expert along to run them), opportunities are more likely to come your way. The American food writer Patricia Wells attended one of the tasting classes I ran at Ladurée and invited me to run chocolate-tasting courses for her too. I became 'Madame Chocolat' at her weekly Friday morning Parisian gastronomic classes.

HOW MUCH DO YOU KNOW?

You may have started this book as a mere chocophile, but already I hope you are beginning to feel more of an affinity with the product. How many of the following questions can you answer that you couldn't before?

- Where do cocoa trees grow?

- Which trees produce the most aromatic beans?

- What are the three main production steps from bean to bar that are crucial to the final aromatic quality of the chocolate?

- What are the ingredients of a dark chocolate bar? A milk chocolate bar?

- What are the ingredients you should not find/feel in a fine chocolate?

- What makes bad chocolate (make a list!)?

- What does 70% cocoa mean on a label?

- Why isn't white chocolate really chocolate?

- What is the best drink and food to go with chocolate?

- List at least five criteria for a good tasting session.

- What is the percentage of Criollo cocoa used in world production?

- Why should chocolate and coffee not be served together?

- How often do you try new chocolate?

- Do you attend chocolate clubs, and read about chocolate?

- Do you choco-surf on the web?

Feeling as if you have some level of expertise in any subject – particularly one about which you feel passionately – is great for your self-esteem. It can also change your life, introducing you to new people, and new activities (holding chocolate-themed parties, attending or hosting chocolate tasting workshops, and reading the news from international events, even if you cannot attend them in person) – and even if it doesn't turn into a career, as it did for me, it can only bring a new and special dimension to your everyday life.

For the ardent chocolate lover, I can think of no better time than now, when we are in the middle of a chocolate revolution, to further your knowledge and expand your interest. After years of living in the chocolate wilderness, we are seeing major changes that will make history, as happened in the 1850s with the Swiss and Dutch technological breakthroughs. There is much to learn and much to keep abreast of if you are to play an active role as a connoisseur and be part of this revolution.

CHAPTER 10

·

The future of chocolate

*T*HE CHOCOLATE REVOLUTION isn't happening in isolation. We are in the middle of a quality revolution in all food and drink. Look around you. Quality ingredients – or at least labels that suggest quality – are everywhere. Suddenly everything is 'boutique'. Even supermarkets know their suppliers by name (or so they say). Farmers' markets are springing up for people wanting to buy direct from the producer. Boutique wineries are now on the tourist route in countries like Australia and Italy. The local continental deli still exists, but has competition from gourmet delis selling top-quality luxury products from around the world.

And chocolate is no different. People are, at last, waking up to the fact that variety of cocoa beans used, and the way they are treated after harvest and processed in the factories, can greatly influence the flavour and texture of a bar of chocolate. We are starting to see the difference, even in our supermarkets.

But, just as cosmetics manufacturers may seize on the fashion for ingredients like aloe vera or green tea and add these words (and perhaps a hint of the essential ingredient!) to their products, even the big, mainstream chocolate manufacturers have been quick to recognise the new trend for chocolates made with beans from a named country of origin. And they have also been quick to recognise the cachet associated with a label stating such information.

As a connoisseur, you can help to ensure that chocolates pertaining to be quality products really are just that, and not just the same old products in a new, trendy package. By buying selectively, and demanding the best, you can make a difference to the world of chocolate.

MAKING A DIFFERENCE

In my own way, I try to make the world of chocolate a more honest, and ultimately a better and more enjoyable, place. I try to show people how to distinguish poor from good quality by having them taste both at the same time, as you've learnt to do in this book. Often people find the difference so striking that it immediately triggers a change in their shopping behaviour.

And sometimes I see small changes that I may have helped to bring about in the chocolate world — as the result of a conversation with a manufacturer, or by having the idea to introduce a few people who could have a lot to offer each other.

One of the most touching moments for me came in 2004, with the release of a new bar that I had helped bring out. In July 2003 a man working for a company based in Papua New Guinea came to see me, bringing three bags of beans from his plantation. He wanted my opinion on them, as he'd been told they were of high quality, and had read about me in the press. I'm far from being a bean expert, so I suggested he contact a few companies that I know are always on the lookout for quality beans.

A few months later I received a long thank you letter and a cocoa-harvest sculpture. One of the brands I'd suggested had liked the beans so much they had signed a long-term contract for them, assuring the village they came from an improved income and secure future for the next few years.

And the brand? It was the French company Michel Cluizel, and they launched Maralumi, their fifth plantation bar, in September 2004. It felt wonderful to have helped not only the world of chocolate but also a small village.

Signs of the revolution

There are many important changes taking place every day, more signs of the choco-revolution. Let's look at a few of them now.

New flavours

Now that you are becoming aware of the different flavours in chocolate, you may be pleased to hear that some companies are reducing the often overpowering amounts of vanilla flavouring in their chocolate or replacing vanillin with real vanilla. In the future, I hope that the amounts used will be much more discreet, just as sugar should be – just enough to hold the aromas and allow them to express themselves with elegance, while maximising their potential.

In fact, when the American company Scharffen Berger produced a batch of Jamaica chocolate just for Fortnum & Mason, they reduced the vanilla on my request – and I am keeping my fingers crossed that the next new bar I see from them will be vanilla-free! Domori is another company cutting back or not using vanilla for most bars. Others, such as Claudio Corallo and Steve de Vries, don't even consider using it in the first place.

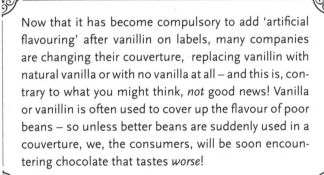

Now that it has become compulsory to add 'artificial flavouring' after vanillin on labels, many companies are changing their couverture, replacing vanillin with natural vanilla or with no vanilla at all – and this is, contrary to what you might think, *not* good news! Vanilla or vanillin is often used to cover up the flavour of poor beans – so unless better beans are suddenly used in a couverture, we, the consumers, will be soon encountering chocolate that tastes *worse*!

In the future, people will not be so surprised when finding flavours of mushrooms, wood, prunes, jasmine and leather in chocolate bars. They will describe a bar as some do wine, speaking about aromas and flavours and their evolution over time. They will compare vintages, and be suspicious if, from one year to another, two different vintages have the same taste.

New style labels

The first thing to appear on our chocolate labels was its percentage of cocoa solids, then exotic words such as Criollo and Trinitario started to creep in – telling us what kind of tree the beans that made our chocolate came from.

Another change that has gradually been taking place is that percentages, once announced loudly on the front of a label, have been disappearing, or rather, have moved to the back of many labels, becoming just another item in the ingredients list. Now, instead, we are seeing the names of countries, regions or specific plantations, and sometimes even followed by the year of the bean's growth – similar to the 'cru 2004' (vintage) you would find on a wine label.

In the future the name of the particular bean used, such as Criollo, will only be legal on the packaging if genetically checked and crossed with an accurate location on the map of the plantation the beans come from.

As you know, pure Criollo disappeared a long time ago, and brands mentioning this bean are in fact talking about a hybrid of Criollo and Trinitario beans. Fine chocolate makers have tended not to use the word at all. But companies such as Domori, Pralus and others are planting pure Criollo (sourced from gene banks and grafted onto Trinitario roots), and waiting for their trees to mature. In 2003, the first bar made with pure Criollo beans appeared – Domori's Puertomar – and there will be many more to come.

The new labels, once you have become used to them, provide you with much more information – and the more you taste and try different bars, the more you will be able to pick and choose from the bars of the future exactly which ones you are likely to enjoy.

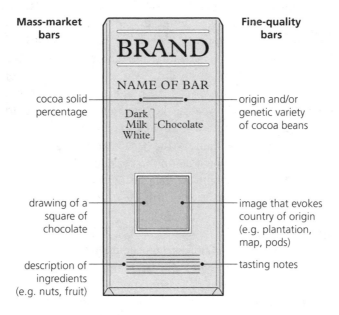

Mass-market bars

cocoa solid percentage

drawing of a square of chocolate

description of ingredients (e.g. nuts, fruit)

Fine-quality bars

origin and/or genetic variety of cocoa beans

image that evokes country of origin (e.g. plantation, map, pods)

tasting notes

BRAND

NAME OF BAR

Dark
Milk —Chocolate
White

Characteristics of mass-market chocolate labels are on the left and those of fine chocolate labels are on the right

Tasting notes on bars

Now that you know that two bars of chocolate, both with 75% cocoa content, can taste completely different, you probably won't be surprised to know that more and more bars present tasting notes on the back of the packaging. I am confident that in the near future, this will become the norm!

Use these notes as a guide, but don't take what their authors say for granted. Use your own nose and palate to tell you what to add to your database. In fact, I suggest that you taste the chocolate for the first time – and read the notes later. And don't feel bad if you didn't taste the same flavours!

In the future, labels will be clear and informative at the same time. The main focus is likely to be the tasting notes. At present these tend to be very simple (often only giving just the 'family' flavours, such as fruity, spicy or flowery, rather than more complex and detailed flavours). A new trend at the moment is to give a 'shopping list' of many different flavours. How can so many flavours exist within the one bar? My advice is to trust your own developing judgement.

CHOCOLATE IN THE NEWS

In January 2004, I discovered a revolutionary shop in San Francisco: Fog City News. In this narrow little newsagent, newspapers actually only occupy a third of the space, and the rest is packed with hundreds of chocolate bars – brands from all over the world, including many of those I cherish. Every taste was catered for, from top of the price range bars of Amedei and Valrhona, down to mass-market products such as Lindt and Cadbury Fruit & Nut. Amazingly enough, despite having a better range than many chocolate shops, and with two-thirds of the shop invaded by chocolate, it is still known as a newsagent!

What's even more astonishing is that when you buy a bar, you can ask for advice – all the sales staff are fully choco-trained! Not only this, but you can ask for a printout with a description of the product, its brand name, the percentage of cocoa and tasting notes. Wonderful!

Curious to compare with my own methods, I asked for a sample printout. I went for one I know by heart, my beloved Manjari from Valrhona. I read:

Flavour: Raspberry, faint pineapple, orange zest, balsamic vinegar, dried cranberry, vine, espresso, green olive, green bell pepper, paprika, nutmeg, oregano, cedar, spicy cinnamon, clove, condensed milk, sarsaparilla, walnut, rum, white raisin, oak, maple, rose, anise, vanilla, mint.

Aroma: whiskey, pipe tobacco, tangerine, stronger cinnamon, honey, blueberry, cedar, fresh cut wood, lemonade, BBQ sauce, Worcestershire sauce, wheat bread, dried cranberry, candied ginger.

Phase 1:
White pepper, clove, sourdough, raisin, ginger, tangerine, lemongrass, lime, celery, apricot, nutmeg, cranberry, beeswax, cucumber, ginger, strawberry, cedar, marzipan, paprika, and a raisin finish. Aftertaste of orange marmalade, tangy blueberry, mocha, sourdough, raisin, long aftertaste of citrus-y fruit.

Phase 2:
Maple, clove, peppercorn, rose, cinnamon stick, vanilla, orange peel, sweeter this time, almond cookie, coconut, vanilla, pear, apricot, burned espresso, pear skin, ripe kiwi, finish of lime. After-taste of toasted vanilla bean combined with orange peel, molasses, pine cone, pine nut.

Wow! Tasting is a very personal thing, and everyone will have their own way of describing a bar. Personally, I think it's better to have only a few short words to guide you on your way – but I do find this approach excellent. At the very least, these notes are suggesting a new way to look at and taste the bars. Use the suggestions as inspiration, and you might even agree with one or two.

New names

As in the fashion world, it is the true craftsmen who are always ahead of the game. The most creative artisans will always be taking risks and being more innovative than the largest companies, who will ultimately copy their ideas (although, in my opinion, only to produce an inferior imitation). But of course by the time they launch their copy, the creatives will already be working on new products. It's a familiar story – just think of the high-street knock-offs that hit the shops soon after the catwalk shows.

It is down to us, the consumers, to seek out the genuinely fine-quality products and not wait until a bar of Chuao is as easy to find as a Gap T-shirt.

In Chapter 1 I gave you my tips for wonderful chocolate brands. I've also suggested a few names to watch out for in the future on pages 26–29 – most of whom don't sell to the general public yet, or do so only in limited quantities. These artisans are not well known at the moment but they are likely to influence even the largest companies in time. Here's a reminder of those rising stars:

- Domori: you can already buy their chocolate, but now some of it is made from Criollo beans – with every year bringing more Criollo bars.

- Steve de Vries: Steve's chocolates are still in the experimental stage, but his 'experiments' have been so far the best chocolate I've ever tasted. He is one of those pushing the boundaries, and we are bound to see more of him.

- Claudio Corallo: his chocolates are ground-breaking and becoming more readily available. Unusually, he both grows beans and produces chocolate – and so can control the whole process.

And in the world of bonbons, there is Jacques Genin. He is nothing short of a genius. His flavours and techniques again will prove hugely influential.

The price of quality

Next time you go shopping, pay attention to the changes. Look at the range of prices you find for chocolate bars. Yes, chocolate bars – not boxes. With the trend towards quality growing, it is becoming more and more accepted that, just as with wine, you can pay prices ranging from the rock bottom to the very top.

In the case of 'limited edition' chocolates such as Valrhona's plantation bar Gran Couva which was launched in 1998, the number of bars available for sale was directly related to the size of the harvest, and chocolatiers bought them in advance to ensure they'd have some for their customers.

And often, with rarity comes price. In 2003 the Belgian chocolatier Pierre Marcolini launched a bar labelled 'Limited Edition' in huge letters, selling for almost $16 for a 3 oz bar! An American radio station even put expensive chocolate on the news, reporting in 2004: 'In Hawaii, one factory owner is selling bars for $7 each – and they're flying off the shelves.'

But is it merely fashion? Not at all. I say get ready: things are just warming up. In the next few years I think that there will be chocolates available that are the result of years of intense research and a little bit of genius. And also during this time period most of the pure Criollo bars that Domori have planned to launch since 1995 will come to fruition (see page 27). I think it's likely that the prices of some bars will soar. For the most exclusive bars created from the most care-fully selected beans, prices per 3½ oz may rise up to $90 to $150 according to scarcity. (You laugh, but it happened with olive oil and balsamic vinegar!)

Digging for gold

Now that there's this movement towards quality chocolate, governments are discovering the marketing potential of their cocoa beans – and this is good news for the connoisseur.

Venezuela was the first country in the world to wake up and smell the beans, supporting the creation of the El Rey brand. This makes Venezuela one of the only bean-producing countries to also manufacture its own finer-quality chocolate onshore and export it successfully. But what of the others?

Colombia was swift to notice how successful Venezuelan bean-growing has been in recent years, and decided to revive cocoa growing in the state of Santander, eastern Colombia. They have been growing cocoa here for more than two centuries, with small and medium-size farms supporting 12,000 families. On the side of the Venezuelan border lies the highly regarded region of Lago Maracaibo. Both Domori and Amedei use beans from this region. In addition, Columbia also has its own chocolate producer – even if in my estimation, it is not yet quite up to standard. Look out for Chocolates Santander, though, as they are actively working on improving their techniques.

Ghana also boasts a rare manufacturer, Omanhene, which produces chocolate from beans grown in the country. Their bars are very popular in the USA.

I do hope that the example of these few countries will be copied by other cocoa producers, lest they lose all their beans to overseas producers. Most of the money is in the grinding and producing of chocolate, not in the growing of the bean. It is sad to see many quality brands using beans from Venezuela for their plantation bars, using names of the regions that have become synonymous with quality – and making profits that the Venezuelans don't see much of. (In fact, only 17 per cent of the total price you pay for a mass-market bar comes from the cost of beans.)

Most of these chocolates are not great quality, but for many, a bar's origin will be their main criterion for buying it. This is a form of fair trade that will have more and more success. As soon as their aromatic and textural quality reach good levels, I will be happy, and proud, to carry them at Fortnum & Mason.

And what about my own country, Mexico? Currently, there is nothing exciting to report, but I am full of hope. As the country with the oldest and most interesting cocoa background, it has a ready-made, explosive marketing tool. Mexican TV was eager to showcase the Mexican chocolate buyer recruited by Fortnum & Mason, and a few months later a leading chocolate manufacturer sent me samples, asking for my advice on how to improve their range. Mexico may yet become a chocolate 'name' again, and I hope to see action taken to revive its plantations and support the development of a local industry.

Status-symbol chocolate

Ten years ago, almost no chocolate manufacturer or chocolatier had ever visited a cocoa plantation. Today, it is the trend. And some particularly adventurous ones such as Pralus, Domori, Amedei and Steve decided to buy land and grow their own beans. Rather than buying the finest-quality raw material, they will ensure that they have it – by growing it and caring for it themselves. And the great news is that many of those doing this are growing Criollos. It's wonderful for us – it means that the quality of chocolate as we know it now is likely to get even better in the future.

Now that chocolate is gaining status, its packaging is becoming more like that of fine perfume. Labels or brochures tell the story behind that product; a map shows where the beans come from. Tasting notes guide your tasting, and information on the brand's philosophy allows you to position them among the others.

ALL THAT GLITTERS...

Beware! As I mentioned in Chapter 6, where there is demand there is always a cowboy lurking around the corner, ready to lure you with a fake. An expensive-looking package, carrying all the right chocolate vocabulary, and backed by a strong advertising campaign, might look alluring – but inside the wrapping is the same old thing you have always been able to buy. The only difference is the pumped-up price.

Be ready for their fancy names and wrappings. When glitter and gold are sharing the same shelf space, you need to be able to spot the difference.

Just keep an eye on what pops up in the shops, and buy a bar here and there, as connoisseurs need to be up to date with the market. Trust me: just a sniff should be enough to make you realise you're on to something special – or that you should push that brand aside for the time being. For the next five years, stick to the brands on the right-hand side of page 33.

And if I have my own way...

Chocolate liquid, kept at 45°C (113°F) will be delivered door to door by big tank trucks. In the homes, sinks will have two taps: one for water, one for liquid tempered chocolate.

Restaurant menus will routinely offer, as they do for cheese or cakes, a trolley filled with a selection of the finest chocolate bars. The waiter, the chocolate equivalent of a sommelier, will suggest an assortment of five or six. Of course, this will be served as a starter, not at the end of the meal (when your palate is less fresh).

Shops will have a reduced range of bonbons to give more space to a wide choice of bars, classified by bean region and variety. Perfectly trained sales staff will guide you to your choice. In exclusive shops, you will be able to book an appointment with the chocolate buyer to get a 30-minute choco-analysis session, at the end of which you will have a personalised list of bars to buy and a new appointment booked in a month's time.

Agrotourism will extend to the chocolate world. Imagine a week's holiday spent on a plantation, getting to know the harvest, seeing fermentation and drying, making your own chocolate and designing the label. Your friends will be impressed!

Coffee shops will no longer serve squares of chocolate with their coffee and if you are nostalgic and ask for one, they will look at you as if you asked for salt – or ketchup!

And by the vending machines at train stations, in offices, and public places, there will always be a selection of top-quality chocolate squares, milk and dark, for your daily fixes.

That may sound like a fantasy world, but look at the changes we have seen in cheese, wine, tea, coffee and olive oil. Thirty years ago, who would have predicted the range of produce to which we now have access? Chocolate is even more of a fantasy food, and it fires the imagination unlike anything else I know of. So are my ideas for chocolate really so offbeat? We shall see…

Ten things you really need to know about chocolate

1. To the Mayas chocolate was a gift from the gods (and this is reflected in the Latin name for the cocoa tree: *Theobroma cacao*, meaning 'food of the gods'). But since mass market production began in the nineteeth century, chocolate has not been treated with much respect. Little care is taken over its fermentation and drying, and processing has focused on changing its flavour rather than enhancing it.

2. Manufacturers quickly seized upon a sweet, vanilla-flavoured product that humans were programmed to like – and they rubbed their hands with glee, watching the money roll in. Today ninety per cent of the world's chocolate is produced by a few large companies. Even those chocolates that seemingly hail from bijou chocolatiers may, when you examine their ingredients, come from one of the big manufacturers.

3. Now the truth about chocolate has finally been re-discovered: when farmed and processed with lots of tender loving care, it is a fine and fragrant food. The world's most aromatic beans are now finding their way into exclusive bars, and experts are taking genetic material from fine trees to ensure a better future for the special varieties like Criollos, which had disappeared until a few years ago.

4. When you taste one of these chocolates it can spark a story or image in your mind – it is truly heavenly, and its aromas and flavours say far more to you than any marketing device ever will.

5. You won't find these chocolate bars in your average sweet shop or supermarket – not yet anyway – and will have to seek them out, looking for specialist shops and internet sites.

6. When you start to eat this chocolate, taking the time to savour it away from other food and drinks, you will gain more satisfaction from it, learning to eat it in moderation, and only consuming what your body needs – so you can eat all you want without guilt or fear of weight gain.

7. Your new chocolate regime will mean having to store different types of chocolate to suit different moods and times of day – you will now have the perfect excuse to go on a chocolate shopping spree!

8. As you become acquainted with more chocolates, you will become more selective, eventually rejecting the sweetest chocolates of your childhood.

9. As you become more selective, you will be better able to recognise the impostors as big manufacturers try to jump on the connoisseur bandwagon, with clever marketing to make their cheaply produced chocolates look more special to the consumer or to your local chocolatier.

10. As the demand for true quality grows, all manufacturers will eventually be forced to look at their processing techniques and see how they can improve their product. There will be more call for special beans, and buyers will be stricter about quality control. And, the best news of all? Chocolate will be back where it belongs – as a respected and revered food of the gods.

A last word…

*B*Y NOW YOU probably know that being a chocolate connoisseur is a matter of degree. You have learned a great deal about what chocolate is (and isn't), and what makes good-quality chocolate stand out from the rest. You know how to taste it, and quite a lot more about yourself and what you like.

You also know that being passionate about chocolate takes dedication, devotion and perfectionism. I have met experts in tea, coffee, perfume and wine; and, it is no accident that after just a few minutes together, we recognise each other as coming from the same planet. When we talk about our particular passion, we shine. And we are here to alight this passion in others. We are driven by the same values, the same mission: to lobby the world about our passion. For chocolate, the new revolution is underway.

Glossary

AOC (Appellation d'Origine Controlée): in English, meaning 'guarantee of controlled origin'. The French initiated the AOC system to safeguard the quality and guarantee the provenance of grapes used in certain wines. This concept is now being adapted for use in the world of chocolate.

Ballotin: the 'ballotin', a gift box for chocolates, was first invented by the wife of Belgian chocolatier Neuhaus in 1912.

Bloom: a condition affecting the surface appearance of chocolate (it looks dull or grey) due to migration to the surface of sugar (because the chocolate has been exposed to excess humidity) or cocoa butter (too rapid a change in temperature, preventing proper crystallisation). A sign that texture is damaged, but with little impact on taste.

Chocolatier: a French term for chocolate makers who either produce chocolate from the bean or melt bulk chocolate to make filled chocolates (the vast majority).

Cocoa beans: the beans inside cocoa pods, the fruit of cocoa trees.

Cocoa butter: 50–55% of a cocoa bean's weight represents cocoa butter. If kept below 18°F, this fat looks and feels like yellowy-white soap. Many chocolatiers add cocoa butter to increase viscosity and give chocolate a smooth texture. As it is expensive, in poor-quality chocolate it is partially replaced by other vegetable fats.

Cocoa liquor: when cocoa nibs are milled at the factory, cocoa liquor is produced. At above 104°F this paste has the consistency of peanut butter and is beginning to smell of something like chocolate. The cocoa liquor is pressed to extract the cocoa butter, leaving a solid matter called cocoa presscake.

Cocoa nibs: cocoa beans that have had their shells removed and broken into small pieces.

Cocoa pods: the fruit of the cocoa tree, containing around 50 cocoa beans.

Cocoa powder: is obtained by crumbling cocoa presscake.

Cocoa presscake: the solid matter that remains after cocoa liquor has been pressed and cocoa butter has been extracted.

Cocoa solids % (also referred to as cocoa content): represents everything that comes from cocoa beans – that is, ground cocoa beans as well as added cocoa butter. A high cocoa solids percentage does not imply strong choco-late. For example, a chocolate labelled '70% cocoa solids' could contain 2 oz ground beans + ¼ oz added cocoa butter. It could also represent 2 oz ground beans + ½ oz added cocoa butter. As cocoa butter has no taste, the latter would be weaker in aromas and would have a more fatty feel.

Conching: process that consists of a machine kneading the chocolate mixture for up to 3 days at a temperature between 140°F to 167°F. Acidity is reduced and aromas develop.

Couverture: most chocolatiers buy chocolate in bulk, called 'couverture', rather than grinding their own cocoa beans. Couverture can take the form of ready-to-melt chocolate, in big blocks of 2 to 55 lbs, or chocolate which has been pre-melted and tempered, delivered as a liquid.

Criollo: the finest and most aromatic of the three species of cultivated cocoa tree. As it is the most vulnerable to disease and has the smallest yield, it was replaced in the twentieth century. 'Criollo' on packaging, if not a lie, refers to the 'modern Criollo', a hybrid of Criollo and Trinitario. Since 2000, a demand for aromatic quality has triggered its revival in this form.

Dark chocolate: to be called 'dark' chocolate has to contain no milk powder and a minimum of 43% cocoa solids (35% in the USA).

Drying: once fermented and drained, cocoa beans are dried in the sun or with hot air. This reduces humidity to less than 6–8%, preventing germination and reducing risks of mould during storage and shipment.

Fermentation: a natural process which occurs when the cocoa beans, still covered in their fruity pulp or mucilage, are put in wooden boxes and mixed every 5–7 days. This brings out the precursors of the aromas which will be transformed into aromas at conching.

Forastero: one of the three species of cocoa tree (close to 85% of world pro-duction). They have the least aromatic beans but are disease-resistant with the best yield. Found mainly in Africa (but not Madagascar).

Ganache: mixture of cream and chocolate, found in all truffles.

Lecithin: an extract of soy beans. It is an emulsifier which is added to choco-late mixture to help achieve the right texture.

Mélangeur: this is an old-style grinding machine.

Milk chocolate: milk chocolate has to contain a minimum of 25% cocoa solids (10% in the USA). Its is enriched with milk powder and usually has more sugar than dark chocolate.

Nibs: *see* Cocoa nibs.

Percentage: *see* Cocoa solids.

Plantation bar: a bar made exclusively from beans selected from a plantation of a few acres, usually renowned for the quality of its beans. Similar to *Domaine* for wines. Plantation bars began in 1994 with Hacienda el Rosario from Bonnat. Aromas vary from one vintage to another and editions are limited.

Porcelana: a single genetic variety of cocoa beans, with more than 90% of Criollo genes, which comes only from Sur del Lago, Venezuela.

Praline: a Belgian word used for all filled chocolates.

Praliné: the French word used to describe a chocolate made with a mixture of roasted almonds and/or hazelnuts ground together with caramel.

Presscake: *see* Cocoa presscake.

Roasting: cocoa beans are roasted to bring out the aromas of the beans.

Shelling: a winnowing machine is used to remove the shells from the beans to leave what are known as the cocoa nibs.

Single-estate/Single-origin: a 'single-estate' or 'single-origin' bar indicates that the cocoa beans used to produce it are from a specific region of a country (like 'Bordeaux' on a wine label) or a single country.

Tempering: the process of careful heating and cooling that produces dark shiny chocolate with a sharp cut. The cocoa butter in chocolate has six crystal forms; tempering evenly distributes mainly the fifth form. Untempered ot poorly tempered chocolate is dull, streaky and often grainy.

Trinitario: the Trinitario is descended from a cross between Criollo and Forastero. This tree has hybrid characteristics – robustness, aromatic beans, and a fairly good yield.

Vanillin: a cheap synthetic version of vanilla.

White chocolate: this is not legally chocolate as it is not made from cocoa beans. The main ingredients are cocoa butter (often other fats are added), milk powder and sugar. The taste comes from the milk powder and the added vanilla (or vanillin), thus the quality of a white chocolate relies on their quality. White chocolate is confectionery, not chocolate.

Bibliography

Aftel, Mandy, *Essence and Alchemy: A Book of Perfume,* San Francisco, North Point Press, 2001.

Bailleux, Nathalie *et al., Le Livre du Chocolat,* Paris, Flammarion, 1995.

Boynton, Sandra, *Chocolate: The Consuming Passion,* London, Methuen, 1982.

Coe, Sophie D. and Coe, Michael D., *The True History of Chocolate,* London, Thames & Hudson, 1996.

Khodorowsky, Katherine, and de Loisy, Oliver, *Chocolat et grands crus de cacao,* Paris, Editions Solar, 2003.

Prescilla, Maricel E., *The New Taste of Chocolate,* Berkeley, Ten Speed Press, 2001.

Robinson, Jancis, *How to Taste,* New York, Simon & Schuster, 2001.

Robinson, Jancis, *Jancis Robinson's Wine Tasting Workbook,* London, Conran Octopus, 2000.

Resources

*A*S WITH ANY TOPIC, the internet has become the easiest and fastest way to find out about chocolate. Over the last five years, chocolate-related websites have mushroomed. Although these are 'international', be aware that shipping constraints and costs, as well as the storage conditions of the chocolates as they wing their way to you, can make this an expensive option. So I strongly recommend that you surf websites of companies or organisations whose headquarters are in your own country. Below I have listed some useful websites, which I have divided into categories. You can subscribe to email newsletters through many of the websites, and these will keep you informed about choco events or the launch of new products.

Research

www.icco.org – the website of the International Cocoa Organisation. It provides statistics and annual reports on cocoa-producing countries and all sectors of the industry.

www.retailconfectioners.org – is rich in information on legislation, retailers and brands in the USA.

Online Shopping

www.amedei.it

www.chocolateco-op.com (UK)

www.chocolatesource.com (USA)

www.chocolats-pralus.com

www. chocophile.com (USA)

www.cluizel.com

www.domori.com

www.intveld.de/english.htm (Germany)

www.recchiuticonfections.com

www.valrhona.com

Chocolate clubs

Do use your internet search engine and type in the words 'chocolate clubs' to look up others that may appeal to you more – or are simply closer to where you live.

www.chocolate.co.uk (UK)

www.croqueurschocolat.com (France)

www.passionnes-chocolat.ch (Switzerland)

www. seventypercent.com (UK)

Index